Listening
FOR
God's Silent
Language

Other Books by Don Osgood

Listening FOR God's Silent Language

Hearing God Speak IN THE *Unexpected Places of Life*

DON OSGOOD

BETHANY HOUSE PUBLISHERS
Minneapolis, Minnesota 55438

Published by Bethany House Publishers
A Ministry of Bethany Fellowship, Inc.
11300 Hampshire Avenue South
Minneapolis, Minnesota 55438

ISBN 1-55661-530-2

Printed in the United States of America.

To Joan,
and our four sons:

———— ⌘ ————

You are the five most precious gifts
of life and love on earth.

And to the silent love of God:

———— ⌘ ————

Now I see and hear it all around me.

DON OSGOOD is president of the Career Performance Group, a management consulting firm, and a motivational speaker for corporate and professional organizations. He is the author of nine books and serves as a board member for several large organizations. He and his wife make their home in New York state.

CONTENTS

THE BEGINNING

It began with four simple words, spoken to me by a maintenance employee in the hospital where my son died:

"See God in everything," the man said.

He spoke the words quietly, lovingly. And my life began to change.

It was a quiet change—not like a thunderclap startling me into action, but a seed falling into loosened soil and quietly sprouting. Slowly those words began to work in me . . . and I began to look at even the simplest events of life with new recognition.

For years, I had wondered why life was so easy for me when others were experiencing losses and hard times. I had also wondered how I would handle my own loss of a loved one. Would I be strong? Would I lose my faith and my other relationships, or would adversity strengthen my trust in God and my love for those who were dear to me?

My father died first that year. Then my son, one month later. Now, deep in loss, I seemed to hear an answer in that wise man's words. Or if not an answer, then, hope. A way to continue.

"See God in everything," that messenger said.

In the months and years to come, I began to follow his prescription. And as I looked, I began to listen, too. I began to hear God's silent language all around me.

I suspect that God at times refuses to speak our language in the imperfect way we command our tongue, bound as it is with our human imperfections, the way we use it to train our children or require others to communicate with us. He speaks another language that requires us to listen harder, to look for His silent work in our lives and the world around us.

And it's not because God doesn't want us to understand. It is because He knows that the effort we put into understanding moves us closer to Him—and to one another.

It is a little like going to Paris, where it helps to try to speak French or at least to listen to the language. When we watch and listen and imagine—when we put ourselves in someone else's place—we get out of ourselves and into a new world, an enriching one we hardly noticed before. To understand what a Frenchman is saying we need to understand a Frenchman's heart.

And that is how I believe we must learn to understand the things in life that aren't spelled out for us. We must learn to see what isn't readily apparent, to hear and interpret the language of another world. And to do that, we must first assume that we are always being spoken to, that in some manner God is always communicating with us, from His heart.

As I began, haltingly, to take that hospital maintenance man's advice, I began to assume God was indeed speaking to me—that His work was there for me to see. I wanted to learn from my experience, but I didn't know what I was supposed to learn or in which direction I should grow. So I began to look for ways to change my environment or my perspective of it, to discern what I was supposed to do with the rest of my life.

My question was not a desperate one, "How can I live?"

It was a searching one, "How shall I live?"

Not an angry demand, "Why don't you come right out and tell me what you want, God?" Rather, a decision, "I must understand what I am now being told. I must learn this silent language. I must keep looking until I can see God in everything."

So without a textbook or a language school, I set out to follow that wise man's advice. To try to see God in everything, to hear His silent language in the many voices around me—both in those of other people, and those among God's larger creation.

This book tells the story of my quest to look and listen. I tell it in the hope that it will help you to sense the patient working of God in your own life.

Because my circumstances are different, the ways I have come to hear God speaking may also be different. For instance, I inherited from my mother a love of the road, and my business makes frequent travel necessary. So many of my most meaningful discoveries have been made in planes and trains, in looking out at the great scenery of the world. I am male, married, a parent, a business consultant, a Congregationalist—and all these things may make me different from you.

But no matter what your life is like, I believe that God is speaking to you all the time. He is communicating in the unique circumstances of your life. And while His language may occasionally come as strikingly as a neon sign flashing a brilliant thought into your mind, more often he will require you to peer into the darkness until you sense the unmistakable presence of God.

So I invite you to come with me on a seeking journey. Assume that God is now speaking to you in all the events of your life, even as you read this book.

If you look and listen closely, while you read, I believe you too will hear a message of comfort, beauty, and growth.

Part One

WHAT LOVE REALLY IS

1

TOGETHER ON THE CLIFF'S EDGE

A JOURNEY WITH JOAN

"Be subject to one another out of reverence for Christ."

—Paul's Letter to the Ephesians

"Good evening," the voice on the loudspeaker says. "This is American Flight 104, bound for London. We'll arrive tomorrow morning at 7:50."

It is an unusual time for Joan and me to fly to London. Only a handful of passengers share the cabin of the wide-body Mc-Donnell-Douglas MD–11 as it thunders down the runway and lifts away from Kennedy International Airport. It is Thanksgiving night. Who wants to travel on Thanksgiving?

But for Joan and me this is one of our serendipity trips, a time to get away, grow closer, make new discoveries together. And even though we try to make this kind of getaway a regular practice, this one is different. We are finally going to the Holy Land, a double discovery for me. Ever since Joan decided she wanted to be someone else, we have needed to keep closer to each other, and I have needed to get closer to God.

But when Leslie dropped us off at Kennedy, I noticed something was missing.

"Joan, the garment bag!"

"What? It's not in the trunk?"

"I can't find it. All our evening clothes. It's not here."

We look at each other as Leslie looks on, no doubt expecting an argument. But Joan just raises her eyebrows, and I see no need to assign blame.

With someone else, I might have wondered if a suitcase left behind were merely an excuse to shop in a city like London. But Joan has never been that way about shopping, and lately she hasn't had much time even to think about clothes. Ministers of the gospel often work harder than most people know.

"We've got fourteen hours in London before we fly on to Tel-Aviv," she says, her gift of good-natured humor in high gear. "Maybe we can find some clothes there. No need to let a little thing like a lack of clothes spoil our trip together."

Our real trip together started when we were very young, during the Korean War. I said, "If we get married now, maybe I can bring you overseas after I get there. I hear I'm not going to Korea, so it just might work." I couldn't see losing a girl like that. Her brunette curls, her quick dimpling smile, her dark brown eyes that caressed me in her look. She was the most exciting girl in the Catskill Mountains.

So I left her at the old Schenectady, New York, train station just one week to the day after we were married. I looked at her just before stepping aboard the heavy black train, waiting impatiently for our hard goodbye. "I'll send for you if I can." There were tears in her eyes as I held her. "It's only been a week, Don." The train jolted, then pulled us apart.

All the way across the country I kept trying to convince myself that I would see her soon. But I didn't know where I was going. For fourteen days across the Pacific on a lonely troopship, I propped up my desolation with my plan to bring Joanie to our first home somewhere in the Far East.

When I arrived in the Philippines, I saw my plans wouldn't work. "I can't bring you after all," I wrote. "I never thought it would be like this. It's too dangerous, even though we're not in Korea. It's a secret base, and there's nothing much here but jungle, mud, and native villages." In the dark, crowded nights in Japanese barracks left behind by their retreat, I learned to invite Joanie into my dreams, to see her smiling at me, to hear her saying words I needed to hear. Seventeen long months—learning to listen to the silence.

Being apart so long was an unlikely way to start a successful marriage or to keep it successful. But somehow it worked. We had encouraged each other by our daily letters. We had refused to let a wartime separation spoil our romance.

After those long months, my train rumbled into the same Schenectady train station. She was standing there silhouetted in the early morning light looking for me. But at first I didn't see her; I turned to go down the stairs. "Don!" she called out, and seventeen months evaporated in a long, passionate kiss with a forgotten duffel bag lying on the cold cement floor.

Chapter one of our life together was written with pure romance. Later it turned toward growth as we raised our four sons, balancing the hectic life of an IBM career with growing family needs, then conquering the challenges of building a business and starting a new career. Now our marriage has turned to companionship—a sense of togetherness forged during our time of tragedy—what most people would call the ultimate family tragedy. Somehow we managed to survive that, making the fact that we forgot our garment bag such a little thing.

Now, looking out my window at the graceful wing of the MD–11, I admire the slim, swept-back curve of shining metal that ends thirty feet from my window. The wing sports a rakish sixty-degree upturn at the end, where the wing light sends a silent, blinking message to the world.

"Look . . . out. Look . . . out. Look . . ."

As the wide body lumbers down the runway the wing floats up and down, and I think, *What a fragile thing!* When we are airborne there'll be a lot of strain on that tip. The wing is going to be stretched up even farther if it's going to bear this huge load.

But the wing doesn't do a thing. The wheels leave the ground, announcing their departure with a soft thump, and the fragile wing stops its quavering. It stands straight out without a quiver as the big silver luxury liner swoops out over the black Atlantic, rising as boldly and improbably into the dark of night as our marriage did forty-one years ago.

Arching left in a wide, graceful turn we cross the fat part of Long Island, leaving a long chain of shore lights behind and passing another line of lights as we leave Long Island Sound behind and thunder out over Connecticut. Joan has already found an empty row of seats in the midsection of the cabin and stretches out for a rare evening of sleep across the Atlantic. A different loudspeaker voice breaks through the steady hum of the big jet engines. "This is your captain. Shortly you will see the lights of Providence, Rhode Island, off to the right."

Just like our marriage, I think. Providence. Somehow, God has always provided—and we've learned how to receive it.

The captain's voice interrupts: "We'll pass over the Boston area, then out again over the North Atlantic on our way over Nova Scotia and Newfoundland before landfall over Northern Ireland. Then we'll continue over Manchester in middle England and on to London's Heathrow Airport."

I look over at Joan, sleeping through the announcement. She deserves a deep sleep. It's been a hard few months.

Looking at her, I think how different she is from me. And how we both have changed.

Forty-one years, and now she's a minister. Not me. Not the minister's son who people assumed would follow in his father's footsteps. How surprising life turns out.

The flight attendant is standing quietly beside my seat. "What would you like for dinner this evening?"

"Oh. Dinner. Yes." I point to the menu card she handed out earlier. "This, I think."

She smiles as though I had selected the best possible choice. Somehow her smile makes me feel appreciated, respected.

She places the meal on my tray table, then says, "Let me trade with you. This one has a larger filet."

Now I'm smiling inwardly. Being cared for is such a basic part of life. It livens up any relationship, whether it's a forty-one-year marriage or a forty-second introduction.

I look at the filet and the description on the menu: "Filet mignon with sun-dried tomato, basil butter, and potato wedges." I settle into the flavorful meal while Joan sleeps peacefully across the aisle.

We have no business taking this vacation. Business is slow. Joan is recovering from a throat infection. We're leaving our sons and their families on Thanksgiving Day. And then there's the flight attendants' strike, the eternal unrest in Israel, the terrible connections, now no evening clothes for the conference. Is someone trying to tell us something?

But my prayer was, "If you want us to go—if our marriage needs something—overcome all this, please."

After dinner, I stretch out on another row of six vacant seats and sleep fitfully through the night, waking to the thoughtful voice of the flight attendant. "Ladies and gentlemen, a good morning to you. We're sorry to disturb your rest, but we have just passed over Manchester. In a few minutes we will make our approach to Heathrow."

Swinging up and peering over the row of seats, I blink a look through the left windows. The brilliant orange of early morning is already stabbing out into a clear blue sky. I think of the worldwide wonder of sunrise. Since our son died, I can no longer simply watch a sunrise or a sunset. Watching Jeff's life flicker out, I began to take unexplainable notice of the simple gift of seeing the morning light and the evening sun.

Joan slips back to me from her row of seats and hands me one of the breakfasts she just received from the flight attendant.

"What would you like to drink?" she asks, rested, alert, loving.

The big MD–11 drifts down through the London mist toward the runway, then roars up sharply at full power. We just missed a collision, I think, knowing from years of world travel that something is really wrong. It takes about two minutes before the captain is able to recover fully and explain in his cultured, soothing voice: "By our sudden ascent you know we've changed plans—just a shift in visibility at ground level, that's all."

He sounds like the doctors at Sloan Kettering Hospital in Manhattan years ago. "Your son is comfortable now. His sedation removes all the pain. We've got everything under control."

But they didn't. Not the cancer. Not Jeff's life.

"It often happens this way over Heathrow as the sun comes up."

Uh-huh. Nice job. Smooth talk, Captain. I wonder what really happened.

But within twenty minutes we are on the ground. We take the London tube to Hounslow Central Station and a small hotel to rest up. By three that afternoon, London time, we are awake and setting out into the fog to find some clothes.

Our fourteen-hour stopover turns out to be one of those miniature serendipities, those little nuggets of togetherness that make a marriage come alive again, turning a foggy day into excitement—shopping at Debenham's, laughing together as we locate just what we need, buying snack food in a little London delicatessen and eating it in our room, watching the London news before taking a brisk walk to catch the tube back to Heathrow for our 10:40 night flight. The electronic sign lists it: "British Air Flight 0660. Tel-Aviv. On time." Unconsciously we stand close as we look at our gate.

Romance. Growth. Now companionship. Companionship is underrated. It can transform a forgetful moment, a left-behind garment bag, into a shared day of triumph.

BA 0660 is the last flight to Tel-Aviv out of Heathrow tonight. As the Boeing 767 roars down the runway, lifts up over misty London, and breaks into the dark, clear sky, Joan and I settle into dinner together and a movie with just one set of earphones. We could get another set, but we like the intimacy of sharing.

As we fly through the night toward the Holy Land, I remember a sign I saw back at Heathrow. Its message applies to our marriage—to any marriage. It said, "Don't wait for the future. Go out and make it happen." And I realize that we have somehow managed to make the second chapter of our marriage better than the first. Still there's something we must learn.

I ponder that as our Boeing 767 slices through the night air at thirty-two thousand feet—over Geneva, down the western length of Italy all the way to the heel of the boot, then across the tip of Greece and the island of Cyprus, winging our way to the Israeli sunrise. What is it that makes one marriage last for forty-one years when others plunge like a jet falling out of the sky—leaving wisdom like a forgotten garment bag left behind in the closet of our lives?

Most of the passengers have settled down for a brief doze while the plane hums its way across the Mediterranean toward Tel-Aviv. They don't see the rose clouds of morning lighting up as we approach the Israeli shore. As we descend into a world we have only read about, we are soon to see an enduring heritage come alive. We are about to learn the intimacy of our history.

In Bible times a part of today's city of Tel-Aviv was called Jaffa. It was the scene of Jonah's escape by ship before he was swallowed by the great fish prepared by God. It was the place St. Peter stayed overnight, at Simon the Tanner's house, where God showed him a vision of a table spread so that Peter would know he didn't need to abide by all the old laws of life that made so much sense, or was it no sense?

Simon the Tanner's house is still there in Jaffa. And so are all the enduring laws.

But what is it in our marriage that endures in these days of high-speed technology, of movies viewed in a luxury liner, traveling at five-hundred-sixty miles an hour? What is important? Who is important? What has held our lives together? Will we hold together the rest of the way?

It was three years after our marriage that the first of our four sons was born. We wanted to have a girl, too. But each son turned out to be what we needed, and loved. And then, much later, there was a young woman named Leslie in our lives. But long before our family of boys, and Leslie, when my Air Force tour came to an end, when Joan closed out her banking career, we moved back to our home area, to IBM when it was just growing into the modern American business marvel.

And that was when my career began to take over. A promotion to the Washington, D.C., area. Then another promotion, to corporate headquarters. World travel. Grown sons. But along the way, long before it lost its grip on the computer industry, IBM began to lose its luster for me. Once rooted in Judeo-Christian values, IBM became a religion (pagan at that) instead of a company, and I began to see what was happening. I searched for the right moment to leave, to start over in my own business.

So at the thirty-year mark I walked out without a job, without a contract for my new firm, without anything except a compelling desire to restart my life. My IBM managers asked incredulously, "Why would you want to leave IBM?"

"I just need to discover something," I said, knowing they wouldn't understand. None of us knew then that IBM would soon nose-dive.

"Don't wait for the future. Go out and make it happen." I knew that line long before I saw it in the London airport.

The changes continued, and the changes rippled into surprises as my new business took hold. Our oldest son, Kevin, decided to leave IBM also, after only three years. He moved into a contracting business. "I've been losing touch with my family, Dad," he said. "I want to make sure I watch my children grow." I understood. But then Joan began to question, "What is there for me to do now that the boys have become men and Don has started his new business?" And what happened in the next few years was harder for me to understand.

I came in one evening, and Joan said, "I went for a walk today, and my friend asked me a question." Joan was trying to tell me something important. I looked at her, waiting, and she looked back at me, closely.

"I told my friend that I want to do something with my life, but I don't know what."

"Yes? What did she say?"

"She asked me something that took me by surprise, Don. She asked, 'If you could do anything you want to do, what would you do?' "

"And what did you tell her?"

"I said I'd like to go to divinity school."

"Divinity school! Why?"

"I don't know. I'd just like to go. There's a divinity school an hour and a half from here, at Yale. I could drive there every day."

"Yale! That's one of the most liberal divinity schools in the country."

"But I'm not liberal, and it's so near."

I knew she could do it. She had always done well at anything she decided to do. I really would have lost her if we hadn't been married before I went overseas—she would have found someone else. But now she had become a wise and loving mother of our children. She also became an accomplished singer as a member of the classical singing group that later became the well-known Washington Oratorio Society. She sang with the Paul Hill Chorale, too. Joan was finding that she could do just about anything she set out to do. She had completed her undergraduate work after the boys had grown up, and she was ready to conquer a new mountain.

But I had a problem. It wasn't Joan's problem and it wasn't Joan. It was me. What do you do when your spouse changes? When your life partner doesn't want to be the person you married?

It was not really a new question, though. We had begun to face that a few years before. Ten years earlier we had enjoyed what seemed like a nice little arrangement. Unspoken but understood. It was a pedestal pact. I was the breadwinner, the successful provider. She was the housewife, mother, the talented person who could do volunteer work in just about anything—give piano lessons, teach Sunday school, whatever was needed. She supported me on my pedestal; I supported her on hers. But then she decided she wanted to step off the Christian housewife pedestal, to go back to school, and head for a career.

She was saying, as she would say a few years later, "I don't want to be what I've been."

She didn't want to do something different, she wanted to *be* someone different.

We continued to make sure we did things together. And one night it was a movie with a Cinderella and Prince Charming theme. Halfway through the movie I could see that the romance we were watching was going to end happily ever after. But I also felt a powerful message inside. Our marriage was not going to end happily ever after—at least not like that movie. Joan didn't want to be Cinderella any longer. So I realized I couldn't be Prince Charming anymore.

Right there in the middle of Radio City Music Hall, in the middle of a movie, I understood the real crisis. Sometimes God breaks through the roof of a theater and gives us a message.

We took a little drive the next day, one of those serendipity trips we had started taking years before. I said, "The movie last night showed me something. In the middle of it I felt that you don't want to be Cinderella anymore."

"I don't."

It was hard to see this change in our marriage—something I thought would never change. When one person in a marriage changes, the other must change in some way or the marriage is headed for a cliff.

My change meant that I had to step off my own pedestal. But that's a big step that seemed a long way down, and I was afraid.

"I . . . I felt you wanted to change . . . last night for the first time I understood it . . . in the movie."

We drove on in silence.

"Now I feel something else."

"Yes?" She was looking at me.

"I feel . . . you don't want me to call you Joanie anymore."

"I don't."

I drove on, not knowing how to handle what was going on. This was Joanie. She had been Joanie to me since I had first known her, when she visited the parsonage where my family lived. My father was the new pastor. She was a junior-high-aged girl, a new convert, and she had come to welcome the family. Even then, I noticed her dark curls and her radiance.

This was the teenaged beauty who agreed to marry me even though she knew I had to leave for overseas a week after our wedding. This was the beautiful young wife who had waited for me at the Schenectady train station when I finally came home. The one who had gone everywhere I was assigned to go while I was in the Air Force, and later when I was moved around the country by IBM.

Now she was saying, "I'm not that person any longer."

On the outside she looked the same to me—beautiful, bright, her affectionate smile always there.

But inside she was no longer the person I married. And she

was asking me a question I had not thought would ever be a part of our relationship. She was asking, just by her decision to be someone else, whether I could love the new person she had decided to become.

Her words were straightforward.

"I love you, Don. I just want to be Joan, not Joanie. Can you love me for who I am now, not for who I was?"

I couldn't speak and I didn't want to listen. Our unspoken understanding was that we would always be the same. Did she have a right to change who she was? or our marriage? But was I different? Had I changed the deal, too?

The silent miles we drove were life-changing miles as I quietly turned over the most important thoughts I had considered in years. All the other business and family notions had been absorbed from others around me. These were my primary considerations now, from deep inside.

What is important? Who is important? Where are we going?

I never wanted to lose her. But I had already lost what we were. Could I love the new Joan as much? Could I love her when she wasn't who she was? But, again, was I who I had been?

I looked over at her, patiently waiting beside me as we rode on. I tried to get the words out, but they were stuck way down in my emotions over what we had been together.

"I . . . I love you . . ."

I knew I couldn't say her old name anymore. It wasn't her.

"I . . . I'll call you by your new name. But I need some time."

"How much time?"

"I need a week . . . to call you that. It's so hard to call you that."

There was no backing out now. Either I loved the new person sitting beside me or I lived in yesterday, in a yesterday that no longer existed. With a person who no longer existed. But I knew one thing. I wanted to love her. I wanted to love the new . . .

I looked at her again. "I love . . . you. I . . . love . . . you."

I tried again, forcing out the word.

"I love you . . . Joan."

It was one of the hardest sentences I ever spoke. Not the love part, the Joan part. It was giving up yesterday. I was growing, and growing can be painful. There is risk in change and in all real relationships. But there is no relationship without risk.

That breakthrough in our marriage happened years before Joan's announcement that she wanted to go to divinity school. It set the stage for me to realize that divinity school should be her decision, not mine. Joan had become my wife, not my student, not my responsibility to bring up, not my property. I needed to respond as her husband, not as an interpreter of her theology.

When we change our perspectives earlier in our marriages our new perspectives become stepping-stones for later-life decisions. To gain a new perspective, our questions must be simple and profound.

What is important? Who is important? What are we going to do about it?

So Joan went to Yale, and I continued to wrestle with a new idea—for me, about successful marriage. We don't own the people we love. We are not to own our spouses, our parents, even our children. For eighteen years or so, we are to decide things for our sons and daughters. We are to train them, be lovingly strong with them. But we don't own them.

We are never granted the option of owning anyone. Nor does God own us. Because He knows that owning isn't loving. He chooses to let us grow without wanting to own us, though He *could*. Loving is giving, not owning. And love is the force that gets us through change, through the most trying changes that come to us. We change by letting people we love change, by giving up, not by holding on to yesterday.

But it isn't easy to let someone close to you change, especially when you feel someone else—or something else—is changing the person you love. Just as IBM had changed me and Joan had not liked it, Yale was changing Joan, and I didn't like it. With all we had learned together, this change seemed deeper still. It tampered with our fundamental beliefs—about God, about men and women. It was becoming no longer a question of whether our love would grow, it was a question of whether our marriage would survive the intrusion of another force that was changing our relationship.

There seemed no solution to our emerging divergence. Standing in the middle of our kitchen one morning, we faced the moment of critical communication over fundamental beliefs that bonded us years before but now were driving us apart. The teachings of Yale Divinity School were raising profoundly disturbing questions. Is God man or woman? What is man's role and woman's role? Who are you, Joan? and who am I?

The romance in our marriage was leaving now, and the growth in our marriage was stalled. We had not yet learned that the growth of a marriage requires *both* partners to grow. While one discovers a new insight, a different approach to life, even an altered belief, the other must grow in understanding, wisdom, patience, even if he or she can't agree. Love allows change, gives up its own way, but that doesn't happen easily. Growth always hurts a little. Sometimes a lot.

We stood in our kitchen that morning looking at each other, caught by some force that was about to destroy what a young marriage with a wartime separation could not, what corporate haughtiness did not, though these had caused some struggles.

We were on our own now, as all marriage relationships ultimately are. We were facing each other across the small floor space between the kitchen sink and the refrigerator, but really across the wide divide of my focus on success in a new business and Joan's focus on a new set of ideas fostered by a seminary. We were slipping toward disaster. Groping our way, trying to hold on to what had worked before . . . but now it was hard to find what was still there.

"So . . . that's the path for you, is it?"

"It is."

"Then maybe you should follow your own path and I'll follow mine."

"Maybe so."

"Maybe we should sell the house, split the equity, and walk our separate ways until things settle down." I'd heard that bit of popular wisdom, knowing it had ended in disaster for many others, but now I was repeating it. We had the choice of going away or facing the underlying issue.

Without saying it, Joan and I were deciding whether we could face this change together.

It was a tense moment. A moment for growth in our marriage

or for irreplaceable loss. We had groped our way to the edge of a cliff, we were standing on the point of no return. But there was still an inch of space, an instant of time when one word could turn us around. And it came. One word.

"No. . . . We don't need to sell our house to work things out."

"Oh?"

"No. This is our place. We bought it together. We remodeled it together. It's ours."

"Yes . . . that's right."

"So we can stay right here. We've been together a long time. Maybe we can learn how to get through this."

It was a huge moment, stepping back from the crumbling edge. Nothing was really settled—all our disagreements still hung out there in the air. And yet somehow everything was changed—inside.

I remember these things as British Air Flight 0660 wings its way toward the Holy Land, closer to the extraordinary balance of love and conflict that exists in the city of God, Jerusalem. Somehow, after teetering precariously on the edge, Joan and I managed to step back, to find balance, too.

We gave each other permission to grow, to be different, and that set the stage for a new chapter in our marriage.

Our minister, Dr. Nate Adams, had once advised me to look at marriage as a matter of being subject to each other instead of constantly asking "Who's in charge here?" Now it seemed to me that God must be in charge of our marriage if it was going to work.

So, tentatively, yet decisively, we began laying the foundation for a new and more beautiful blending of romance, growth, and companionship yet to come.

It was right at this juncture that the most tragic event in our lives happened. This one event made so strong an impact on our marriage and our lives that I can only attempt to describe it. It was the kind of life-and-death experience that can drive a marriage to a bitter end or renew it with inexplicable growth.

Somehow, with God's grace, we managed to grow.

But that is another chapter.

2

ONLY ONE LOVE

A LOST AND FOUND MYSTERY

"Love bears all things, believes all things, endures all things. Love never ends."

—The first Letter to the Corinthians

Night passes swiftly when you fly into the sunrise. The rosy clouds of morning are lighting up the east as we approach Tel-Aviv. It seems I have barely had time to doze as BA Flight 0660 raced across the Mediterranean. But I have had plenty of time to think—about sunsets and sunrises, about the inexplicable mysteries of love and death and relationships lost and found.

It was my bittersweet privilege to be with my son Jeff on his last night of breathing by himself. You realize how strong your love for air is when you see your son suddenly lose it.

Over the past few months, as Jeff lost the privileges of open windows and of nature's textures—even of eating—I had begun to pray with new appreciation for simple joys. "Thank you, Lord, for the taste of food. Thank you for grass, for sunshine, the feel of the wind against my face. For the sunrise."

But I had not yet recognized the miracle of air. We can gulp down huge lungfuls of it, and its supply never ends. It is a lifetime gift we spend most of our lives overlooking.

But not Jeff. Not that night.

We were alone that evening for a reason I did not know in advance. I had felt I should stay overnight again with Jeff, camping out on the floor beside his bed, just to be there. Suddenly, about midnight, I realized he could hardly breathe.

"Something's . . . gone . . . wrong," he said between labored breaths. I rang for the nurse, who gave him a dose of something and assured us the medication would quickly resolve his discomfort.

For forty-five minutes Jeff fought for air, holding his arms out to the railings to expand his lungs. Finally, I realized the nurse's assurances had been faulty. Jeff's pleading look tore me inside.

When I found the intern, he gave Jeff 100 percent oxygen, but outside the room he cautioned me. "I can't keep him on 100 percent oxygen for long. He will be damaged by it." Then he looked at me and said, "Anything can happen, you know."

I knew.

We had been preparing for this moment a long time . . . or it seemed a long time, though it was only three months. Is there ever enough preparation time for losing your son?

The call had come in the early evening. Our younger son, Drew, answered the phone, then turned it over to me.

"Dad." Jeff's voice was urgent. "I'm in the doctor's office. There's something wrong. The doctor wants me to go to the hospital right now. I can't even go home."

He never did go home.

One day he was a young laser scientist, happily married to a talented nurse. He and Lindy were enjoying their first home, looking forward to the future. The next day he was a cancer patient—probed, cut open, treated with round after round of chemicals that sapped his strength even as they sought to control the rampaging cells within him.

Week after week he had rallied, declined, gained ground, lost it. And now the doctors were telling me that a breathing machine was the only hope.

———— ⁓ ————

I went back to Jeff, who was breathing in precious oxygen. He said, "Dad, will you pray with me?"

Standing by Jeff's bed now, after three months of standing by, I had no more words to pray. We had prayed all the ways we knew how to pray, as had hundreds of people across America.

What does a father do when his son agrees to go on a breathing machine and knows more than you do about what that means?

"We will need sign language, Dad."

"All right."

"This means I'm OK. And this means I'm not," he said, gesturing in the air.

"Yes," I said, looking closely at his improvised signs.

"This means Lindy, and this means Dad, and this means Mom."

Now, standing by his bed to pray after discussing the signs, I knew spoken words were just as limited as those few signs. All I could do was recognize that I had no power at all to say what I wanted to say. Words of encouragement were empty. There was only one word that seemed powerful enough.

"Jesus," I said. And then I reverted to the memorized songs I had learned when I was a boy at home in a Wesleyan Methodist parsonage.

"Jesus . . . is the sweetest name I know," I said. "I see you, Jesus. We see you, Jesus."

I was consciously turning to someone who knew more than I did about suffering, to the One my father had turned to and his father had turned to. Both were ministers. Both had died of cancer in their beds at home—my father just a month before. Had he seen the same power I was seeing now in my prayer?

Dad, where are you now? I miss you, Dad.

In that moment I felt someone come up behind me and over to Jeff, lying at my left. I was so startled at the swiftness of the person who had come in that I looked to Jeff's side. Amazingly, I saw no one. Jeff was looking at me and must have seen my look of dismay. In my confusion at not seeing the reality of the Presence

31

there, I couldn't look any longer. I just bowed my head silently, not noticing that Jeff had become someone different.

Then I felt Jeff's fingers reaching mine and weakly squeezing them.

He was comforting me.

"Will you stand beside me, Dad, while I pray?" It was a calm, loving voice I heard, and I moved closer to listen.

"Dear Lord," he whispered, his hand rising up as though on a witness stand.

"Help me to stand by you, Lord, whatever happens."

I could not speak. My son was now stronger than I.

Finally, exhausted, I said, "I'll just lie here beside your bed so I'll be ready . . . when the doctor comes."

"Yes," he said. "You rest now, Dad."

When they came for Jeff, I followed beside him, right up to the swinging doors of the intensive care room. As the doors swung open, I called after him loudly, "I'll be right here, Jeff. I'll be in there as soon as they let me."

Lying on the floor outside the doors I waited, only half realizing the miracle of growth that had been taking place in Jeff. Stretched out on the floor in the middle of the night, I prayed for one miracle while another far deeper miracle was happening.

When the nurse came to me and said, "You can come in now. He's awake," I hurried in, saw the big tube down Jeff's throat and recognized the pain as the nurse vacuumed out the residue from his lungs. The tube was so large.

"Jeff," I said. He coughed.

"Jeff, I'm here."

I desperately wanted him to hear me. I put my hand on his forehead to bless him with my prayer.

"Jesus is here, Jeff. I see you, Jesus," I said, and Jeff instantly relaxed into a deep sleep from which he never moved.

We were never able to use our sign language. So I spoke out loud to Jeff for a week, as we all did. I reached the point of imagining Jeff's prayer and speaking it for him. I became his tongue. His silent language was expressed in an occasional counter breath as he fought the machine. According to the doctors, it was the only way he could communicate. But I knew the heart of Jeff behind the silence.

And it was during this time that the wise hospital maintenance man gave me his life-changing advice.

"See God in everything."

He was telling me to listen for God's silent language. I had heard whispers before. But this was in the hospital. Where I felt the Presence.

During the months of our vigil, Joan and I had moved into the city to be as near to Jeff as we could. Joan dropped out of Yale. I put my business on hold. We stopped our lives.

We returned from the hospital to the New York apartment that night—on the night we knew that our son would die—and we rode up to the apartment in dark despair. We wandered around the living room, looking down at the lights of Kipps Bay, hopelessly, wordlessly asking, *Why are we going to lose Jeff in the flower of his life?*

We spoke words in that dark moment that we could not say to anyone else, words that only the parents of a dying son can say to each other.

"Joan, he looked at me, pleading with his eyes for help."

I was crying.

"No. Don't, Don. Don't say any more."

"But I need to tell someone. I couldn't help him, Joan. I'm his father and I couldn't help him. He looked to me to help him and I couldn't. He was holding up his arms on the sides of the bed so he could get enough air in his lungs."

"You can't tell me this, Don. I can't take this. Why is he dying?"

"God, you can keep him from dying if you want to."

There were other words we spoke, shaken by the coming loss of a life that we had caused to be born. But somehow, somewhere out of that shared misery a new perspective began to dawn. A new resolve to live, to overcome, and to do it together. At no time in our lives had we needed each other more. We knew we must grow from the loss of our son. And out of that loss came a new appreciation for each other.

Without our noticing, our marriage crisis that had no solution slowly died. Just ebbed away as the sunset quietly slips down into tomorrow. The dying of our son and the sunrise on our new to-getherness in marriage occurred at the same time, during those months of growth.

We never really talked about it, though we talked about many other things. It was a fact of life, an intervention from another world. Who can decide whether you'd rather have a son or a mar-riage come back to you? Although the one was not connected to the other as we are able to discern connections in this life, yet the net result of our experience was just that. Our marriage survived the pain of our loss, was strengthened almost without our notic-ing. And in the process, we were spared more than we ever want to know.

We seldom speak of our son. We have never talked of the in-explicable work of God when we lost our son and gained a new marriage. It was too powerful a moment in our lives.

Perhaps I will never be able to discern precisely what hap-pened to Joan and me in those days—any more than I can explain why our marriage grew stronger at a time when so many other marriages disintegrate. Long ago I stopped trying to distinguish exactly where our choices leave off and God's work begins. One rises from the other. As I look back I can see that both made a difference. We chose to reach out to each other instead of pulling away. And God's arms of comfort wrapped us closer together. And somehow in the process, our love, clouded by confusion, fear, and anger, was reborn.

After Jeff died, we encouraged each other. We went on trips together. We took long walks and talked. Slowly, we forged a stronger understanding—and we resolved not to let anything de-stroy our newfound strength.

And surprisingly—to us, at least—our mutual faith deepened through our loss. Its growth took us beyond theological differ-ences. It held us. Neither of us can explain how. Except that any marriage, no matter how it starts, must at some point become holy matrimony.

So Joan went back to Yale to finish her degree and I no longer minded. After our ordeal together, nothing looked the same. I started working again with the clients who had been so patient with my absence. I also founded a personal leadership program called New Perspectives for one of my clients. In it, I focused on the balance we all need between our business and family lives. I included three questions: What is important? Who is important? What are we going to do about it?

And I wrote a book called *Fatherbond*, a memorial to Jeff that began to help even my clients. It touched people as no other book I had written.

Even the potential difficulty of a wife having an advanced degree that put her beyond me in educational attainment was overcome when my alma mater, Houghton College, asked me to accept an honorary doctorate and to join their board of directors. I felt it was just God's way of saying, "I don't want you to let any of the unimportant things get in the way of your marriage."

What makes a marriage grow past youthful romance, past conflict and loss into companionship? I don't know all the secrets, and much of what happened to us is still a mystery to me. But it has something to do with standing beside each other, choosing each other again and again. Learning that what we have can survive anything that comes. Coming to know that commitment can bring love back.

Love is not what we think it is. Love isn't a gift of one person to another. Love isn't even a gift from God. Love is God. God is love. So when He loves us He gives us himself. He can't give us love without giving us himself. That is why we can't give love without giving ourselves.

People keep trying to figure out love. We put adjectives in front of the word to try to put love into understandable compartments. But when we do that, when we label love with terms such as familial love, marital love, brotherly love, even agape love, we water down love. We minimize it by our attempt to define it. The reason we can't define love is because we can't define God.

There is only one love. It is the same love that existed since the beginning of the earth and before that. Love doesn't need to go with anything else. It doesn't depend upon anything else. It is complete by itself.

———————— ∞ ————————

As BA Flight 0660 coasts in from the Mediterranean Sea over Tel-Aviv and settles down in the bright dawn on the runway at Ben Gurion International Airport, we have with us our replacement clothes from London. We are soon to see what it is to arrive on a Saturday, Israel's silent Shabot. The day they say God revisits earth and the nation comes to a stop. By law.

But we are carrying to the Holy Land our pilgrimage beyond law to the source of love, the source of strength. The strong, never-failing love of God himself.

What is important? Who is important? Love is more important than life. Because love never ends.

3

OUR PROMISED LAND

WHAT I LEARNED IN THE JORDAN RIVER

"If a man loves me he will keep my word, and my father will love him, and we will make our home with him."

—The Gospel according to John

"Look out your windows on the right side," the guide says. "We're passing the hometown of Joseph of Arimathea. The rich man who gave his tomb for the burial of Jesus lived right over there, in the town you can see. Arimathea."

We're on the bus to Jerusalem now, rising from the plains of modern Tel-Aviv to the steep hills of Judea. As the guide speaks into the microphone at the head of the modern bus, he pulls us into the past.

"Now, look out the windows on the left side. Jesus appeared here to his friends, walking on *this* road, the road to Emmaus." Our eyes wide, our minds filled with wonder, we look out at history.

"We're about to see the first glimpse of Jerusalem now, and I want to say a Jewish prayer. It is our custom. There is something special about Jerusalem. You will see for yourself. I can't explain it."

Later, we begin to see for ourselves. Even tourist street signs showing maps of the city say, "Pray for the peace of Jerusalem." But it's more than that. It's the history that envelops you, that makes you feel a little closer to God. Or is it the Spirit of God still resting on the many hills of the city?

There's something in Jerusalem that walks around with you, moves up through the valleys with a soft freshness in the air, stands beside you as you pause in the Garden of Gethsemane, cries in you as you descend to the dungeon of Caiaphas where Jesus was left the night he was captured. Something that breathes hard with you as you climb the Mount of Olives and look out over history as you stand on the high hill where Jesus ascended into heaven.

As we stand in the dungeon of Caiaphas I happen to be standing next to a memorial table with a copy of Psalm 88 lying on it. When they ask for a volunteer to read it aloud, I am the natural one. I begin to read a powerful section I do not recall seeing before.

"I am reckoned among those who go down to the pit; I am a man who has no strength, like one forsaken among the dead, like the slain that lie in the grave, like those whom thou dost remember no more. . . ."

I am gripped by the words as I read them aloud to the group. It is as though we are there in the dungeon with Jesus, feeling the same loneliness He felt long ago.

"Thou hast put me in the depths of the pit, in the regions dark and deep. . . ."

There is a stillness as I read on. The rest of the people in the dungeon are listening.

"I am shut in so that I cannot escape; my eye grows dim through sorrow. . . ."

Suddenly I can continue no longer. I am standing where Jesus stood, and my voice is overwhelmed with the realization of what transpired there. The group is patient, praying silently. I can feel their prayers.

One person says softly, "Jesus . . ." Not an oath, but a recognition that we all share. We have reached the place in all the earth where you can understand that Psalm most deeply. A life-changing moment. There will be others.

A few days later Joan and I pick our way through the Arab section of the old city, trying to find a Christian symbol to buy as a memento of our visit. We politely dodge the merchants standing outside their stalls who seek our eye.

"Come and look at my shop. Please," they say.

Turning into a side alley to get away, we stare at a dead end. We are fascinated by the ancient pavement stones underfoot, but we also feel uncomfortable, vulnerable, hemmed in by the foreign-looking stalls crowding into our path and by the watchful eyes of the eager merchants.

We retrace our steps. We turn left and right, searching. Then left, and left again.

I am embarrassed that I can't find our way. It's always been so easy for me. But not now. Have I lost my sense of direction?

Ah! a familiar spot. Relief. "We were here just a few moments ago!"

Another corner now, and in the middle of a crowd, the surprise.

"Joan. The Via Dolorosa! Jesus walked by here." We stand there in silent wonder for just an instant. He labored up this same narrow street with His cross of heavy olive wood on His back. Right here where we are standing.

"My friend!" A merchant reaches out through the crowd with his loud voice. "Can I help you?"

"The Via Dolorosa!"

"Yes. This is it. This is the station . . . seven and one-half." He pats me on the shoulder, smiling. It is his way of having a little fun in the middle of a long day.

It is a day of humility, losing our way in the teeming crowds and winding corridors of the ancient city, but also an opportunity to feel much as visitors must have felt over the centuries. To realize that all of us are pilgrims to somewhere, filled with wonder when we stumble into history just as we were beginning to feel hopelessly lost.

But that is the way it works when we try to get closer to God by our own sense of direction. We think we are wandering aimlessly when what we are looking for is just around the corner.

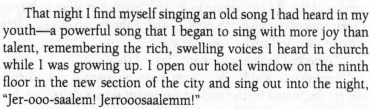

That night I find myself singing an old song I had heard in my youth—a powerful song that I began to sing with more joy than talent, remembering the rich, swelling voices I heard in church while I was growing up. I open our hotel window on the ninth floor in the new section of the city and sing out into the night, "Jer-ooo-saalem! Jerrooosaalemm!"

I'm not trying to be funny. The guide was right. There's something in the air.

What a feeling to sing that beautiful word out into the sweet evening air.

Jerusalem. . . . Jerusalem. . . .

Jerusalem!

After days of wide-eyed wonder we board a bus for Galilee and wind our way down the steep hills from Jerusalem toward the warmth of the Dead Sea, the lowest place on earth.

On the way we pass Arab Bedouin encampments.

"Joan, look out the right window. Look at the sheep in that old tent yard. And the camels."

"Folks, you are looking out at scenes similar to those from centuries ago. The chief can buy as many wives as he has money for. If he is seventy he can buy a fifteen-year-old wife, just as his ancestors did. Ah, here's a spot. We can pull over here and let you look closer."

Piling out of the air-conditioned bus, we stand facing a Bedouin village. A few black tents stand silently in the sand dunes, alive with sheep and people. An Arab stands by the road, holding his camel by the reins, looking for an opportunity to make a profit. What's new? Semite families will always be in business, even in the desert wilderness.

"Sheckel. Sheckel." That's all he says, softly.

A tourist agrees, and one touch by the Arab, like pushing an elevator button, starts the ancient-looking camel into his slow, patient ritual of kneeling in front, then settling down in back. Coming down! Down please! The camel's slow, fluid motion entrances me as my busmate enjoys a brief, lurching ride.

Back on the desert road, the landscape rolls by. The Dead Sea, where you lean back in the water and your feet pop right up to the surface. Then Masada, the high fortress of mass suicide, where Jews fighting Roman soldiers elected to take their own lives rather than be conquered. A few miles more, Jericho. Did he say the oldest city on earth? You look down into an excavation, and there is part of the unearthed city wall. A corner of Jericho, a part that likely wouldn't have fallen down, a round tower of ancient strength. A man stood there once, placing that rock on that pile. Eleven thousand years ago. Look at that. Look at it!

Behind you, across the valley of the Jordan, Joshua stood, looking over at Jericho, saw a stranger, and asked, "Are you friend or foe?" The angel replied, "I am the captain of the Lord's army," and Joshua immediately knelt before him.

And there, right up there on the mountainside before you, the place where Jesus wandered in isolation in the wilderness. Right there!

On to Galilee. *The* Galilee. The headquarters of Jesus, where Peter lived and fished. Peaceful, beautiful, warm, with palm trees all around.

In moments we are inside the ancient walls of Capernaum, where the ruins of the synagogue Jesus attended still stand in mute evidence of what are now two religions, where the ruins of Peter's house still lie just a few steps away. This is the town where the centurion said to Jesus, likely just inside this gate, right here, and it's almost as though I can hear a voice, "My servant is sick . . . just say the word. . . ." And up there, just around the bend, where we just came from, the high ground where Jesus spoke and someone called it "the Sermon on the Mount." The centurion must have been up there, listening! Must have followed Jesus down here and saw his chance.

I find myself humming softly so no one can hear, "I walked today where Jesus walked." But Joan hears. We are awed by our walk together. Unable to find words for our wonder as we collapse into bed at night, we simply say, "We were there today. I wonder where we will walk tomorrow."

At the end of the next day we stand at the edge of the Jordan

River. We are about to be baptized, though we have been baptized before. This is the moment to go completely under, rather than just have water touch our heads as is customary in our tradition.

One-hundred-fifty or so stand waiting in white gowns, lined up along the bank of the Jordan. This is a special moment. Joan is one of the ministers, shivering in the cool water as we await instructions. I am praying for her.

Lord, keep her warm enough. Protect her. And let her be, out of all the ministers attending here, the one who baptizes me.

The words of the presiding minister drift out over the crowd. "When you go all the way into the water this afternoon, you are renouncing all of your rights. You are renouncing all of your relationships. You are renouncing all of yourself. You are accepting this Jesus whom you have come to know. Jesus who stood in the water of this river and renounced His own rights. You are renouncing and receiving for all time. You are about to be cleansed of yourself, in the water that takes your sins and floats them into the Dead Sea."

Yes. I renounce. And I receive. I draw closer to you, Lord.

The long line moves forward into the water, cold now, getting colder. Up to my waist. Better splash some water on my head. Splash more over my shoulders. Minimize the shock. Can I go through with this? There's someone backing out. "Too cold," she mumbles, wading back.

Now, moving forward in line, I stand beside Ben. Tall, big, smiling, Ben hugs me. He is welcoming me into the water. I know Ben Kinchlow. What a pleasant surprise from this powerful black fisher of men. So this is it. Ben will baptize me.

No.

A staff member's voice says quietly, "You four move ahead, right up to there." Joan is there, smiling at me. Not shivering now, but showing her delight at the surprise. God heard me! Joan will baptize me after all.

Moving between her and another minister, I listen to the words of baptism. I place my hand on my nose, close my eyes, lean back. The refreshing water closes over me. The cleansing of the Lord. It is the supervision of God changing into the Presence of God. By the hand of my wife.

42

Not Joanie. Joan.

How do we get closer to God? How can we get closer to anyone? We can start by sacrificial listening.

By giving up our way, our idea of what is right, our right to our own body. Our right to being in charge. Our right to anything. Our right to everything.

Wherever we are, whether it's in the Jordan River or in some little town in Connecticut or Kansas or California or in the middle of some big city—in the middle of Times Square—we can give it all up.

Then we receive something more. Once we declare we have no more rights than Jesus did, than the King took for himself, we are drawn closer to God. Then, in our inabilities, in our humanness, however gifted, we rely on the sweet presence of God. It's surprising how warm the water is.

A few days later, flying back through seven time zones and seven hours in the air, I marvel at the closeness of God. During a layover of a few hours in England I know it vaguely. But landing in New York I sense it more surely.

Wherever we are, we have the same opportunity for closeness to God. His joy is over all His creation. Over the land now called New England, where we attend church. And over the land where you live, east or west, because His creation includes all the earth. Those who are now growing up in the countryside or the teeming cities have the same gift of closeness, whether they have the privilege of traveling east to the Holy Land or not.

Our Holy Land is wherever we are. We can have a closeness to God whenever we truly want to possess it, without traveling anywhere. Our promised land is where we live, as long as we are willing to move over and share it.

It's not the place. It's not our particular brand of Christianity. It's the unique relationship with God—who comes to us where we live and lives with us.

I begin to understand all this and to feel it deeper as we return home to the beautiful hills and woods of Westchester County. Looking out my window at the quiet stands of trees, the soft-flowing streams and still ponds of Pound Ridge, at a new December snow blanketing the hills and clinging to the trees, I know afresh what I have always known.

He is here with us. He is available.

Speaking His silent language in the flowing water and the falling snow, He quietly declares, "In the middle of your turbulent world I am in control. Listen to me. I am here."

Part Two

TURN TOWARD THE FUTURE

4

IF WE ARE PATIENT, THE ANSWER COMES

A VIEW FROM THE MOUNTAIN

"I came into this world that those who do not see may see. . . ."

—The Gospel according to John

When my father and son died within one month of each other, the same cancer killed them both. They both died bravely, despite the numbing indignities of that disease. During the months of shuffling back and forth from Jeff's hospital room to my dad's bedside in the Adirondacks, I learned the deeper characteristics of love.

About the beauty of serving—as I gave my dad a bath and rubbed my son's feet.

About the lengths that love must go—as I finally agreed to pray with my father that his death would be soon.

About the nearness of our heavenly Father in our pain—as I sensed His Presence keenly.

About the absolute importance of relationships amid all the other pursuits of daily life.

What I didn't learn during those months, what I would struggle to learn over the coming months and years, was how to cope with the sudden absence of my father and my son. How could I live now that a part of me was gone?

"See God in everything," the man had said.

But he didn't tell me how to see God in the empty canyons where love had been. He didn't tell me how to go on with a life that no longer allowed me to see my son and my father.

It was weeks after Jeff died before I slowly began to enter the world of business again, still struggling to find a way to live with my double loss. On my way to business appointments, I hovered between the world of screeching subways jarring my senses and the vivid spiritual peace I had brushed so close to. Those who lose a child know they will never get over it, even feel they wouldn't want to. But one morning I was caught by a startling glimpse of reality that helped me begin to live with a new view.

I caught the early train from Connecticut to Wilmington, Delaware. Gliding quietly past Manhattan, shining yellow in the early morning sun as it waited for the day's swarming commuters, my train arched away, across the East River. I could see the inspiring parade of buildings, looking as though they had marched up the length of Manhattan and now stood at parade rest, mute and glorious in the sun.

My special knowledge of a certain building pulled my eyes unwillingly toward midtown and the familiar outline of a soaring hospital, hiding behind it the smaller hospital where my son had died.

There will always be a spiritual tug when I see that place, alive then with confident-faced doctors, comprising the best that a world of cancer fighters could muster. But they later stood by, powerless and masklike, as Jeff's spirit went quietly up through the floors, leaving his battle for earthly life behind.

Now the hospital was insignificant, impossible to spot, buried among the rise and sweep of Manhattan's buildings as they stretched across my train window like some cinematic scene. Did God really intend that many buildings on one island?

But as I looked at the sweep of Manhattan, perspective came. I saw the little size of that once-important hospital—and the relative smallness of all Manhattan—compared to the depth and expanse of the brilliant blue ocean of air over it. I began to see that we live at the bottom of this ocean, pushing priceless air around between us as we move. When Jeff died he came up through the hospital floors to the top of our ocean—came up, not for air, but to fill his lungs with freedom. Maybe that's why I had felt the unexplainable tugging upward as I stood over Jeff's bed, knowing he was above, not below me.

Now, suddenly, I caught a faint glimpse of another world, as though someone had tilted the train window to reflect a far different place in the Adirondacks, where my father had died.

The glimpse of the Adirondacks, superimposed over Manhattan, showed a towering tumble of mountains and huge, numberless evergreen trees dipping their roots in the water of the Hudson while it was still the clean water of the North River flowing down toward the city.

While the mountain waters streamed down, these giant evergreens had climbed their way up the mountains with glacial slowness, dropping their seeds generation by generation. They now stood on tiptoe atop the mountains, reaching up yet farther into the same blue ocean of air.

When my dad died in his little red-roofed retirement cottage by the lake, tucked in the shadow of one of those ancient mountains, marching on in generations, I realized he had only the attic to rise through before hitting the freedom of the open air.

Swiftly and quietly, he became a part of the mountain's mute history. I was left as seed for another time, beginning to accept that God allows great trees to fall and other trees to take their places on the mountain.

All of that grandeur shadowed the picture in the moving pane. At that moment, watching Manhattan slide by my train window, I saw the spiritual picture I was supposed to see. These giant cities and awesome mountains we wind our way through are only the *places* God loves, some built by Him, some by us. But what He is really looking at is us. The real miracles swarm their way to work and home, not noticing how little the cities and mountains are compared to the blue ocean they are submerged in. I couldn't see anyone looking down on Manhattan, but I could sense the spiritual vision of a God who watches over teeming cities and lonely mountains to find someone who will look up and say, "I see You."

While we watch passively through our framed windowpanes on life trains that rush us through our schedules for a mere twenty-nine years or as many as eighty-six—it matters little the length—we have a brief opportunity to sense the majesty of why God set it all in motion in the first place. Surely He had mutual recognition in mind, not just His viewing us through a one-way mirror.

But can you see God even when you can't see the blue? When you are plunged into darkness?

My train looped back toward the city, rushing at it with determination until we were swallowed up in the darkness of a tunnel. Here, underground, with some people leaving the train before others boarded for Washington and other seemingly important destinations, the engine was unhooked, plunging the cars into darkness. The view through my window was gray and black.

Am I looking through the dimness now to find Him? Is His eye on me? Is He watching, not just an Adirondack attic away, but through the black earth to me?

I sensed an answer. A beginning of an understanding. In the transition from one perspective to another, from one life to another, God doesn't look down on us or through a windowpane at us. Instead, He sits on the seat beside us, saying, "I've been here with you, watching the whole scene through your eyes. Someday I'll give you a chance to see it through mine."

It was a start, a breath of comfort, a promise of hope. For the moment, it was enough. And for the future, a new way to find healing.

I learned to cope with pain on train rides, traveling somewhere away from the familiar, in search of a new perspective. So within two months of Jeff's death Joan and I left town. We even left the United States. Rome, Florence, Venice, and a small resort town on the coast of Yugoslavia helped me begin to watch and listen more carefully. As we traveled I became increasingly aware that there is a message behind many voices we hear, and there is an unspoken spirit within a voice. There are voices to overhear not only in people but in all of creation.

Gradually, I began to understand the messages better. To sense the Presence behind them. To see God in what was happening and what had happened.

In Rome, a priest serving communion at St. Peter's Cathedral didn't know that he was offering something special to two American Protestants on a special journey. The long line of faithful people waiting in the evening for communion among the priceless art and architecture made me more aware than usual that I was about to do something important.

It was the precise moment that I stood before the priest as he spoke two words with extraordinary simplicity and gentleness. "Corpus Christi," he said. "The body of Christ." Nothing more. But there was a silent, familiar Presence within his words that spoke to me, and I heard a remarkable tenderness that touched me in my loss.

The body of Christ. For me.

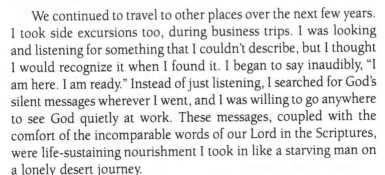

We continued to travel to other places over the next few years. I took side excursions too, during business trips. I was looking and listening for something that I couldn't describe, but I thought I would recognize it when I found it. I began to say inaudibly, "I am here. I am ready." Instead of just listening, I searched for God's silent messages wherever I went, and I was willing to go anywhere to see God quietly at work. These messages, coupled with the comfort of the incomparable words of our Lord in the Scriptures, were life-sustaining nourishment I took in like a starving man on a lonely desert journey.

While in Long Beach, California, for business I saw an advertisement telling of the famous western novelist Zane Grey, who had built a Catalina Island homestead now called the Zane Grey Hotel. "It is as it was," the advertisement seemed to say.

Increasingly, I had found I could understand God's silent language more clearly by the act of writing what I heard. Somehow I felt I might be able to sort out the right thoughts for me in the environment that helped a famous author of American cowboy stories to write with such simplicity.

So I traveled to Avalon—to watch, to listen, to write.

My excursion boat from Long Beach enters the picturesque little harbor at Avalon, and I look for the Zane Grey Hotel above the teeming little resort city. The advertisement described it as a pueblo house, and now I spot it high above the famed Avalon Casino. As soon as we land, I set out for the homestead on foot. Puffing my way up the last steep steps I finally reach my destination, a low, simple-looking pueblo holding fast to a narrow cliff, overlooking the tranquil Pacific on one side and staring point-blank into a desert mountain on the other. It looks like a place that Zane Grey would build.

The man in the hotel office introduces himself as Michael. He is sitting under a huge buffalo head that juts out from the wall behind his desk. A collection of Zane Grey novels are lined up by his side. An apologetic smile breaks across his face when I ask about lunch.

"I'm sorry," Michael tells me. "We have no lunch here. Only a hotel where you can find peace." That word *peace* is a key that unlocks a door to an unusual conversation. Within two minutes we are talking at a level far deeper than I had expected. I forget about lunch.

We discover that both of us are in the process of recovering from loss, and that we both have lost two loved ones at about the same time. He lost his father and mother within two months of each other. The shock made him leave a lucrative business to seek answers on the island, something beyond his Mercedes and his real-estate acquisitions.

Michael's father was a professor of philosophy. My father was a minister. As we talk, we discover that both of us are still hurting from the loss of our fathers. Still looking for something.

"You have not come here by coincidence," Michael says, looking at me closely. Then he adds, "You must go higher up the mountain before you leave. There is a peaceful place higher yet. I go up there to meet nature, and somehow I feel close to my father up there."

I tell Michael about the closeness I felt with my father and my son as they died. But that special feeling has dimmed, so now I am struck by Michael's comment. I respond, "Maybe I can find a spot to do some writing and sorting out."

So now I am leaving Zane Grey's pueblo homestead after barely arriving, sweating my way along a narrow roadway that snakes its way up the desert mountain.

High on the mountain, I arrive at a sharp turn in the road, a place shaded by three scrubby trees. This vantage point looks down on a silent canyon leading to the ocean below. A huge black bird greets my arrival, crowing its way across the desert canyon toward me.

This is the place, I decide. Settling in among the dry bushes, I fashion a comfortable place to write, looking back across the tranquil blue Pacific toward the mainland, indistinguishable now in the California haze except for the faintest tips of the San Bernardino Mountains. In a sense I am looking back in time, trying to recapture the peace my new acquaintance described.

I close my eyes and rest awhile. Then the spell of the mountain begins its work as I start writing. I write for hours, absorbing the feeling of the baked-dry canyon and the enduring, far-off Pacific. The silent language of the vast scene below moves my thoughts, telling me there is something about love, about loss, about what is important and what endures. I begin to describe it better as the sun drops slowly, sending shadows into the folds of the canyon.

Below, on the right and the left, the rocky canyon walls frame the ocean view like curtains on a vast stage.

And now, far below me on the water, the play begins, unfolding in silence like an old-time movie. Far behind the right mountain wall appears a distant passenger boat, aiming arrowlike and silent, back toward the mainland. A moment later another larger cruise ship silently glides out behind the first. But this one, instead of following the first, makes a slow, wide arc toward the west, out to sea. Out toward the future, it seems to me as I watch. The spell of the canyon, the silent movie being played out before me on the ocean far below, makes me listen to a hidden message.

You must get out of yesterday. You must be willing to make a decisive turn toward the future, just as that second ship did.

Slowly it begins to occur to me that I have had trouble moving forward because part of me has been holding on to the past. As if I could somehow keep Dad and Jeff with me by dwelling on my memories of them. As if I would lose them if I let them go.

Now I realize with new freedom: I don't need to maintain that death grip.

"My father hasn't gone," my new friend Michael told me while sitting under the buffalo head in Zane Grey's house. "His presence is still with me; I've learned that up on the mountain." He watched me carefully for signs of understanding as he spoke. "My father smiled a lot," he said. "I see him even now in your smile."

His words struck a deep note in me. The past months I have been slowly waking to this same insight. I, too, have begun to feel the occasional presence of my father and my son after their deaths. Now the understanding flows out as I write, so close to the edge of the canyon.

Our relationship with loved ones who are gone is not really over. A major part of our ongoing grief is in believing a massive lie that love stops when a loved one dies. But that is not true.

Love never dies. Love is always *now*. There is no yesterday in love, and no tomorrow. We need not be content to say, "I loved my father or my child or my mother—once." It is never too late; we can invite love into the present moment. And our loved ones that are gone still love us—perhaps more, because they understand more.

Now, in this silent place, I am moved to speak aloud, to say something that confirms my new understanding. At that moment, the black crow in the same tree above me calls out several times in a commanding voice, as though he is part of the timing of this larger communication. As though encouraging me to speak. And why not? If God can use ravens to feed Elijah, surely He can use a crow to speak to me.

I break the silence of human words with one loud response: "Yes?" I call out. A stranger listening in would think I had mentally gone over the side of the cliff, but the crow cocks his head and looks down. He is listening to me.

"Yes?" I say again, feeling a little foolish. Here I am, talking to a bird in this silent place. Is Zane Grey's desert heat getting to me?

Then I do something different. I speak to the mountain and

to the sea below me. But not really to the mountains and the sea.

"I receive your love, Dad," I say aloud. No one is around to make me feel embarrassed as I shatter the silence. My thoughts are set free now as I speak. "I receive your love, Jeff." Only a breeze from the Pacific below, but I am not discouraged.

"Jeff, I give you my love," I call, loudly now. And the words sound good as they echo into the silence surrounding me.

With these slow-learned words now conquering the silence I begin to break out of yesterday and forget about tomorrow. I have become a part of this moment—reestablishing a relationship with the love I know is there.

So, looking down into the quiet canyon with a cool breeze moving up from the ocean far below, I realize that this abandoned mountain has become a place in which I can give love and receive love, even though no one seems to be around. Now I am in touch with something I have felt without being taught. Or have I received a gift from a mute teacher in the wind?

The Creator of all I am viewing didn't create love and then leave. He *is* love. He came to earth and died and rose again—all because of love. He sent me His Holy Spirit, who makes it possible for us to love each other. He gave me parents to love, a wife to love, children to love. Wherever love is, He is.

I realize that I am beginning to forge a new understanding about God and about death and about love. It is not something I have learned in the churches I have attended—not in so many words. But it is within all the words and actions of our Lord. It is the message in so many passages of the Bible now clearer to me.

This kind of thinking is new to me. It will require more thinking. But for the moment I revel only in the present awareness of love.

Now I am ready to return to the Zane Grey homestead, to say something to my new friend, Michael. Looking at my watch, I am startled into action. Michael is scheduled to get off work in fifteen minutes, and I am still high up the mountain! Can I get back in time to say thank you? Finally, after zig-zagging down the mountain's hairpin turns, hardly noticing the breathtaking views, I bound up the worn steps to the Zane Grey pueblo. Michael is still sitting at his desk under the buffalo head.

"Thank you," I say, with the excitement of my run still in my voice. "I learned something up there on the mountain."

"I'm glad," he answers.

"And there are some good words I saw earlier in the town below. I wrote them down. I'd like you to hear them."

"I'd like that," he says.

So I read to him the words from a sign I saw at a church in the village below the hotel. The words are from ancient King Solomon by way of some Christian descendants of a missionary who started the church there on Catalina Island in 1889. I first heard them long, long ago, but they have come alive for me today, high on Zane Grey's mountain.

> For everything there is a season,
> and a time for every purpose under heaven.
> A time to be born . . . and a time to die . . .
> A time to weep . . . and a time to laugh . . .
> A time to keep . . . and a time to cast away.
> God has made everything beautiful in its time.

Everything beautiful . . . in its time. For me the words fit the Sloan-Kettering maintenance man's words, "See God in everything."

My time was high on a mountainside, looking into a parched canyon, where I spoke to the mountain and the sea, to my father and to my son, to the Creator of all enduring love. For me the answer has come in knowing that love is here now. All we need to do is hold on to it and to remember that love is more important than life. That love never dies—because the God of love never dies. Love flows on forever when we recognize its presence in the silent language of life. We can begin to understand this silent language of love in all the mountains we climb and in all the seas we sail.

There is a time to listen, a time to learn, and a time to do something different, in the beauty of this silent moment. If we are patient, the answer comes, as a soft breeze up the canyon of our souls into our hearts, finally presenting a thought to our minds.

And then we too can answer.
I love you.

It was not a coincidence that I went up a mountainside on Catalina Island. I was called by an advertisement, invited farther up by a new friend sitting under a buffalo head, welcomed by a black bird flying toward me, challenged to speak by an insistent crow. But behind them all a deeper Voice was speaking, and I heard. I was beginning to learn that there are many silent messages and signs in our lives, insisting that we grow into receiving our new role in life. The listening, the understanding, the responding is up to us.

It was not a coincidence that I went up a mountainside on
Catalina Island. I was called by an advertisement, invited farther
up by a new friend sitting under a buffalo head, welcomed by a
black bird flying toward me, challenged to speak by an insistent
crow. But behind them all a deeper Voice was speaking, and I
heard. I was beginning to learn that there are many silent messages and signs in our lives, insisting that we grow into receiving
our new role in life. The listening, the understanding, the responding is up to us.

On that day, on the mountain, I began to know better why I was left to live, what I was called to do next. I needed to set myself toward seeing God in everything, and watching for more opportunities to learn about this silent language I was only beginning to tap. And I needed to reach out to our three sons and practice it with them. All three had been hurt by Jeff's death, but our youngest, Trevor, seemed to be affected most. What would this new language do for him and me, however flawed our practice? I wanted to take a different kind of journey with Trevor, one that started right in front of my home.

5

BUILDING STEPS

A FATHER-SON PROJECT

"Do not provoke your children to wrath."

—The Letter to the Ephesians

My youngest son, Trevor, and I set out to build the stone path together, in steps up from the road, across the lawn to our front porch. It was a summer project that I thought might help Trevor and me work together—a project that would utilize his skills. In a sense it was a business arrangement—I would be paying him. But I really saw it as a way for the two of us to grow closer. What I didn't see was that we would uncover an old problem that neither of us had understood. At ages twenty-three and fifty-eight, we needed to close a gap between us.

"Let's see. Do we start at the top, where it's flat, or at the bottom of the hill?" I asked, revealing my lack of experience. "If we start at the top, we'll be able to lay out the stones in just the right curve between these two trees." I had answered my own question, quite possibly a strategic error. But we started from the porch, agreeing that we would stop where the land fell away, requiring the steps that neither of us knew how to build.

Leaving our curving path of new-laid stones uncompleted at the brow of the hill, we descended to the bottom and dug our way up, aiming for the place we left. I was learning as we went about something called rise and run. It turned out that Trevor already knew this. The height of each step, the rise, needs to be carefully calculated in terms of the amount of horizontal distance you need to cover. If you run too far before you rise you end with an impossible height for the last step. And our reach was clearly exceeding our rise.

Jokingly, we thought of placing a stepladder at the end of the small canyon we were digging, and inviting Joan for a look. "What do you think?" we would ask with blank faces. But before we got the stepladder she walked by and asked, "Why are the steps so far down in the ground?" Her untimely arrival had ruined our stepladder scheme, and when she went inside, Trevor continued joking, "I guess you'll just have to beat her."

Determined to make a good time of it, we clowned back and forth as we dug into the bank, cut railroad ties, spiked them together, laid them out in successive rises, and topped them with two-inch slabs of rectangular bluestone. It was heavy work in the hot sun, but we were making progress. Until my neighbor Art came by.

Art had saved my projects on a couple of occasions, so I listened to him. "If you cut back to an eight-inch rise on each step, you'll stay out of trouble," he said. "You'll be at the right height when you get to the top."

So Trevor went to get some eight-inch railroad ties. As he left he asked diplomatically, "You're sure you want a different kind of step halfway up?"

"Yes. It won't show much." I hated the idea of starting over.

But that night when my neighbor returned I realized he'd meant just that. Start over.

"Make *all* of them eight-inch steps," he urged. "The steps will be there for thirty years, and you'll always wish you'd done them right." He gave his advice good-naturedly, and it made sense. So I tossed and turned a bit that night, wondering how to approach Trevor the next day with the change.

If you want to understand the nature of people, work with them under hard conditions, then tell them they must redo the work, or change the signals in some other way. I knew that from firsthand experience.

I remembered a time, years ago, when I decided to cut down a big tree in the backyard to make way for our deck. I recruited all four of my sons and some neighbor sons, too. We tied a big rope high in the tree to coax it in the right direction. We even had a dry run, an idea borrowed from my IBM experience. I gathered the boys and issued specific instructions. "We'll all pull on the rope until you hear the word, *timber*; then you three run there, you three run right here, and I'll run right over there." It wouldn't do, I thought, to have kids running in to each other while the tree was coming down.

We practiced the dry run to perfection, but that was the end of our glory. The trouble started when I thought I heard my neighbor Art yell "timber." Over the noise of the chain saw I shouted, "Run."

The boys scampered like rabbits to their assigned places, but I fell over the well cap, sure I was about to be crushed under the falling tree. We all watched as the tree tilted in the wrong direction, with glacial slowness, right into the crotch of another tree. Art had not yelled after all. I had given the signal too soon. And we had not been pulling together when we needed to.

The only way to get the tree down now was to cut it from the bottom up, each cut swinging the shortened tree closer to the base of the other tree, until the top finally broke loose and fell away— right on the bow of my sailboat!

But we had survived. We also survived building a bridge together some time later. We didn't really need the bridge, but there was a stream on the property, and it seemed like a good idea to have a path into the woods across the stream. It was a bridge to nowhere with a steep bank on one side and a landing on the other. I invited my older sons to help. My decision to make it a curved bridge complicated things right at the beginning of the project, but we survived that, too. The bridge is there today, arching its way across the stream to a path that leads nowhere in particular, but it is a beautiful thing to see. Unfortunately, that bridge left my older sons a bit skittish about working on projects with me, because I didn't decide exactly what I wanted until we were already building. That spirit of innovation was fun for me but unsettling to them, because they never really understood why we were building the bridge in the first place or where it was heading once we started building it.

Now, years later, staring at the steps Trevor and I were building—half for the steps and half to increase our togetherness, I should have known that Trevor and I were headed for a flap of some kind, because we had elected to meet the top section of the stone walk at a step and on a curve. We were still reaching more than we were rising, even after squeezing the steps from twenty-six inches down to eighteen. Add to this complexity a father and a grown son, each with a mental image of what the design should look like, plus my decision to tear out the steps and start over, and you have all the ingredients of Civil War II.

How do I tell him we must tear out our poor start?

When Trevor arrived the next morning he was the picture of relaxation, steering his comfortable old truck into a spot near the steps, eying his handiwork in the morning sun, looking up at me with a good-natured grin. I summoned my best managerial manner and invited him to sit down on the porch.

"I have something we need to chat about," I said, eying him closely. But no magic words came. How do you make the words, *We're going to start over* sound like an exciting project?

When Trevor heard my announcement he slapped the palm of his hand on his forehead. "Oh no!" he said, "I'm not tearing all that out."

"But look at it this way," I reasoned. "You're getting some good experience for your next customer, and you're getting paid for tearing it out."

"But I'd hoped to get something completed this week," he said, resignation flattening his voice.

"Well, you can go on to another project for a day if you like, before we come back to this one."

"What other project?" he asked, the thought changing his face to a look of worried anticipation.

I breathed a quiet, desperate prayer and plunged in. "I need a small footbridge over the marsh beyond our curved bridge," I said, watching closely for his reaction. Then inspiration touched my lips. "You can have the entire project."

A faint light of hope now flickered in his eye. I could see that we might have a chance if I threw in another incentive.

"I won't even work on the project," I announced magnanimously. That launched him from his slough of despond. He was looking at me now with intrigue in his eyes, mentally hovering over his decision.

"I won't change a thing," I said, still watching him carefully. "I'll just draw a picture of what I want, and I'll let you do it all."

"All right," Trevor said. "But let's get this straight. We draw up everything, and that's the last I'll hear about it until it's done."

"Yes," I said, relieved.

I retreated to my study as another son, Drew, came in, on a break from one of his own contracting jobs. "Trevor's bent out of shape out there, Dad, about the change in the steps."

"I know."

"I told him a lot of my customers change their minds. It's part of the job. We redo lots of things in my work."

"Thanks, Drew. I tried to make it easy, but it isn't so easy."

"He'll get over it, Dad."

Drew and I walked out to the garage and found Trevor just leaving for the lumberyard.

"I'll go with you," I said, wanting to regain some of the sense of togetherness we had felt when we started the project.

"No. That's all right. Just decide in advance what you want next time."

"Look," I said, hurt that he didn't want me along, "you're not the only one frustrated by this. I was wrong. I told you that. It's not easy to face your mistakes. I made one, and I'm paying for it—in more expense, more time lost, and by admitting I'm wrong. How do you think I feel?"

I turned and walked back inside, brooding over my sudden aloneness. I had planned the steps as a way to get together. But now each succeeding step had driven us further apart. What is there about my way of working that gets in the way of togetherness with my sons?

After an hour of waiting I still was perplexed. Finally I decided to retrieve something from the day—by going to see the Yankees play.

Backing out of the drive I passed Trevor's truck coming in. He was searching my face, wanting to say something. I opened my window and heard him say, "I was a little selfish." He hesitated. It was a tentative moment.

"I'm not feeling good about being angry."

Here was a ray of hope. Maybe we could get closer after all.

"Where are you going?" he asked.

"To the ball game."

"Alone?"

"Yes." I hesitated, searching for the right words. "Want to go?"

"Oh, ball games aren't my thing. But I think I can finish your footbridge."

"You mean tonight, or tomorrow?"

"I think tonight."

"Oh." I was waiting, looking for an excuse to stay. But I had already promised to stay off the job.

"See you," I said, and roared away feeling alone. Lonely. Now on my way I began to think: *How dumb I am—driving away from a relationship. Maybe I can just get some fried chicken and come back and we can share it together.*

Now, hurrying back with a box of hot fried chicken, I hoped Trevor would still be there. I wanted to start closing a gap that I still didn't understand.

Ah, Trevor's truck is here. But he's gone.

I walked over the curved bridge my older sons and I had built and down the wooded path to the site for the new footbridge. Seeing no one, I sat down on a garden bench by the stream and slowly ate the chicken, alone. It was quiet there in my clean, green hideaway. Yet I was missing the relationship with Trevor, and I couldn't see the beauty around me.

Crossing the curved bridge and climbing the path by the woodshed, I heard a voice.

"What happened?"

Trevor was there, looking at me, anticipation in his voice.

"I saw that your car was back, but I didn't know where you were." He came down the path as he spoke.

"I decided that going to a ball game was the wrong thing," I said. I should have said, *I missed you and I came back to see you.*

We walked together down to the marsh and the site of the new bridge, and Trevor set about measuring the lumber in satisfied silence, caught up with the prospect of creating something new. I noticed he was drawing a rounded form on the bottom of the lumber. It was now early evening, and the hourly rate I was paying loomed large in my mind. A day had almost gone, and progress on this alternate project seemed to be languishing. The unfinished steps lay in the opened earth on the front lawn in mute testimony that something had gone wrong there. And here Trevor was drawing on the lumber.

"What are you doing?"

"Designing a scallop for the bottom of the bridge."

"But the design we agreed on doesn't call for that. We agreed you'd follow the design."

"All right," he said, abruptly.

He set about building the base for the bridge, and then my neighbor Art came by. He had saved my deck, helped me cut the tree, advised me on the curved bridge, guided us about the steps. I felt I owed him an explanation. With a small grin I said, "We've changed projects for a while. We need a break before we tear out the steps. Trevor is going to build a footbridge."

"If you nail it together here, it may be too heavy to carry across the bridge," Art said. He was just trying to be helpful, but Trevor and I were still trying to avoid Civil War II. Trevor didn't look up.

"I'm just building the base here where it's level," Trevor said. "I'll finish it down there."

"Here's a way to keep the decking lined up," Art said, showing how a piece of lumber could be used as a straightedge. After a short silence, he added, "If you need help to carry the frame down, let me know."

"I think we'll make it," Trevor answered in clipped tones.

I saw that I might possibly be of some help carrying the base, so I waited around. Art went home to dinner, and soon Trevor and I were puffing our way under the load of the base for the bridge, weaving our way down the path, over the curved bridge, and onward to the smaller stream, dropping it over the slow flow of water. At least the water was moving. And so, it finally seemed, was the bonding process between us.

"I can find some rocks for a foundation," I volunteered. "And you can keep on building the bridge."

"All right."

Lugging heavy rocks to the scene, I was happy again, working beside my son, creating something together. *It beats the ball game,* I thought. Then I noticed the decking he was hammering down. He wasn't using Art's straightedge idea, and I thought the slats were off a little.

Guardedly I offered, "The slats aren't straight, you know."

"It's the irregularity of the saw."

I was quiet as long as I could be, watching the slats go down with minute irregularity. "You aren't using Art's straightedge idea," I said finally, as quietly as I could.

"See this?" Trevor said, holding up a short straightedge. "I'm using it."

"No. That's not what he meant. He meant a *long* straightedge."

"This will work as good."

"But it isn't working. The slats are not even."

He stood up, looking away, his back to me. Suddenly he dropped his carpenter's belt to the ground and started away. I knew I had just dropped a nuclear bomb. I started walking back up the path away from him.

"I won't say anything more," I called over my shoulder. "I don't care how you do it. Just keep the slats even."

Stepping across the curved bridge I called out loudly, "You don't listen."

"*I* don't listen?" he shouted back. "*You* don't listen!"

It was Civil War II, and I had caused it. If only I could have stayed away. But I couldn't. I wanted something more than a bridge.

Walking into the kitchen I found Joan just arrived from her office.

We were talking about my frustration when our oldest son, Kevin, dropped in from an evening course at the college. He had made a long detour to our house on his way to his home. I thought, *It's nice when your sons drop by just to talk.*

I was saying to Joan, "Trevor keeps wanting to convince me that he knows how to do the job."

Now Kevin looked at me closely. "Maybe you made him that way. He has learned how to be confident in his approach. He's marketing his skills just as you do in your business. He's like you, you know. Maybe it's something in you that makes you not like what's in him."

I looked at him, caught with the truth of his observation. I thought, *I need to go out and apologize.* But then I heard Trevor's old truck cough to life and creak out of the driveway.

Realizing I was too late, I asked myself again, *How can I close the gap between us?*

Then I had to ask, *What is the gap, anyway?*

Joan looked at me. "It'll work out in the long run, as long as you're both honest."

Catching a train for Washington the next day, I was still thinking of ways to mend the misunderstanding and draw closer to my son. The steps lay unfinished, the new footbridge was undone, and now I had to leave town again. My idea of building steps together and deepening our relationship in the process was shattered. Lonesome again, I listened to the train clicking over the rails beneath me.

But there was a ray of hope when I arrived at my hotel and called Joan.

"Any calls?"

"Yes. Trevor."

I was immediately alert. "What did he say?"

"He said he hoped you would have a good trip and he'll see you next week."

I dialed his number and only reached one of his friends. "Tell him I got his call and I'm looking forward to working with him next week."

Two days later I was home, and Trevor called me. Words of sorrow and apology spilled out of my mouth. "I'm wrong, Trevor. If you'll give me a chance, I'll try to be a better father."

"Don't change too much, Dad," he said. "I'll be over tomorrow."

Excitement bounded up inside of me, as though I were a

twelve-year-old jumping into an old swimming hole. *He'll be over tomorrow!* But I didn't tell anybody my thoughts.

It is the privateness of men not to tell others their thoughts at such a time.

When tomorrow came I met Trevor at the top of the steps. Words have no meaning in themselves, only the meaning of a person in the words we use.

"I'm glad you came," I said, trying to show him my excitement at his return.

We went to work together that day. And we finished those steps wiser than when we started. We mastered the run and the rise and the curved design, and when the work was done we knew we had created a work of strength and beauty. In the process, we stumbled onto a way to talk about controlling behavior between a father and a son. We learned how to talk, a step at a time.

But it wasn't until a year later that I knew for certain that things had worked out well between us. Trevor had come by for a visit. As he was leaving, we walked down the steps together. At the bottom he turned and looked past the flowers that bordered both sides of the curving rise and run. "This is a beautiful job," he said, looking at our joint creation.

"Yes," I said. "But I'm sorry for the pain I caused you."

"Don't be sorry, Dad. We learned something together. We learned to carry on until we were done." And I had learned that the line between getting something done the way I wanted it and empowering my son to use his own creativity was so fine a line that I seldom knew where it was.

It is this line that God has wisely drawn by letting us build our lives without crowding us—without straightedges. God's seeming absence is really His delegation of opportunity to grow. Seeing God in everything includes seeing how God deals with us so we can mend our ways as parents and as people. It is at least a daily necessity.

Trevor and I were grinning at each other now, knowing something we could not have known without building our steps, knowing that we had also, haltingly, taken steps toward each other. And no one will ever take away the invisible steps we took.

Our relationship is the real foundation that lies under the beautiful path we built together.

One morning I looked down on our steps from a second-floor window. There was the graceful curve from the porch winding its way between the two trees, the steps turning and plunging down the hill, twisting right and left and right, passing newly planted flowers on both sides and leveling out perfectly as the walk met the road.

Then I thought of another son who it seemed had been a silent witness to it all. He had helped pull the rope years ago and measured the curve for the bridge to nowhere. But he was not here for the steps, and I didn't want to leave him out. So I went back and visited Jeff's grave, speaking quietly to the wind blowing across the green hillside, "I love you, son."

In one way or another all my sons had helped build our steps, and I learned that building steps *with* your children is building steps *to* your children. If we can't hear someone who loves us— a son, a daughter, a spouse, or God, maybe we should step closer. It is a way to go around the inadequacy of mere words, a way to notice how God would do what we are trying to do. I learned that I had to keep my eyes on God all the way through the project, to keep my ears tuned to His silent language. When I dropped my eyes too long or stopped listening, I got into trouble.

Now I was soon to practice the art of listening and communicating beyond mere words with my mother, as we planned a long trip to Florida before she was unable to travel any more. Already in her late eighties, she had been living alone in her little red-roofed cabin where my father died. I knew she was lonely, and I was lonely for her. And she and I had always shared a love of travel. Now I wanted to take one last journey with her. I wanted it to be my gift to her, my way of serving her.

As is so often the case, she ended up serving me—by teaching me truths I could not have learned without her.

6

RIGHT TO THE WATER'S EDGE

BILLIE'S LAST ADVENTURE

"Honor your father and your mother."

—The Letter to the Ephesians

A long time ago, when my mother was a little girl, she was called Billie because her parents wanted a boy. That name became a pleasant part of her childhood memories, so in her later years I started calling her Billie. It was a respectful name that she liked, a fond tribute to a brave little woman with a quick wit, a constant smile, and an insatiable appetite for adventure. My guess is, it suits her still.

Billie chose to live alone after my father died. And my sisters and I began to feel an unspeakable desire to care for her, to slow life down or find a way to extend her life while she still had the light in her eye. I learned through her love of independence how important it is to live in your own place, to "re-member" yourself with your mate's silent presence and to bow to no one but God.

That is what Clara Osgood chose. And we all stood by her, promising her we would let her stay in her little red-roofed Adirondack Mountain cabin overlooking Long Lake until it became impossible for her to care for herself.

But when is that time? And who will decide?

In such moments of life you quietly dread to become the parent. It's hard to see God in such a reversal of roles.

"I want to stay right here, as your father did," she said. "I still call to him to come to supper, before I remember that he's not here. I go out on my porch swing at the end of the day and watch the sun light up a path of diamonds across the water to the shore below me."

But in separate conversations she confided, "It's hard to live alone."

Now, watching my mother's loneliness slowly sap her will and steal her smile, watching her eyesight fail little by little along with her memory, knowing she should have the freedom to decide whether to live alone, yet concerned about the very real dangers of her remaining alone, I talked with my sisters about what should be done.

Esther said, "I'll never let her leave Long Lake to live somewhere else."

Evangeline said, "I'd appreciate the privilege of mother living with me for a while."

And Marilyn said, "We need to make arrangements so she won't live alone this winter." I had come to feel the same way.

But what do you do when your mother says "no" and your sisters cannot agree? It's hard to know what's right, hard to do what you finally come to believe is right.

That's when I decided to take Billie to Florida. I wanted to see for myself, firsthand, how she was doing. I also wanted to give Billie, always the adventurer, the pleasure of at least one last jaunt.

Billie said, tired and forgetful, "I shouldn't go."

But somehow we convinced her of the value of a vacation. Billie and I flew to Miami, where I rented a car, stowed a rented wheelchair in the trunk, and started off for Key West.

I had second thoughts on the way when I saw how little she remembered and how lost she had become. She wouldn't remember to take her daily medicine. She lost her emergency life-alert pendant, and she needed help with her pacemaker tests.

As we drove she asked, "Do you know where we are?"

"We're in Florida, Billie."

"But why are we here?"

"It's our vacation. It's my Christmas present to you."

"We'd better go back now. I belong in Long Lake."

Oh, Lord, I prayed. *Help me to do right. How am I to return her to Long Lake?*

I had hoped she would turn a corner and enjoy the opportunity to explore. But she had forgotten her joy in exploration. In the motel that night while she slept, I washed her slip. She woke before I did the next morning, and when I woke she came into my room and said, "Someone put my slip in the sink."

"Billie, I was just trying to be a good son."

"Oh. You are a good son," she said. "But can you tell me where we are?"

"In Florida. On the way to Key West." I was despairing now over my failure to help Billie turn around. I walked into the next room. Should we turn back? I had not seen God in this trip. Perhaps I had made a mistake. Then from the next room with the door ajar, I heard her say to herself, "So we're accountable to no one!" There was wonder in her voice, and wonder in my mind as I listened, realizing she had become too dependent over the years and recent months.

We took a walk on the beach that morning. We were at Islamorada, about a third of the way down the long stretch of islands to Key West. It was the first sign of summer for her as we walked in the sun. With the warm breeze in her face, she broke into a smile and spoke such heartwarming words to me. "It's a nice place here, in Florida."

She knows where we are! I thought. "Yes, it's Florida, Billie. It's a warm place."

"As long as we're this far, we might as well go to Key West," she announced.

Ah, this was the old Billie, the explorer with a sparkle in her eye and resolution in her voice. I was exultant! As we drove on toward Key West, it was all I could do to keep my thank-you prayers silent. If I said too much aloud, she'd have known I was worried. She was so quick when she could remember.

Miles down the road she continued to remember where we were. "I think your father and I were here long ago."

"Yes. I remember when you and Dad went to Florida."

Another mile or so went by. "I don't remember that we made it all the way to Key West."

"I don't know, Billie, but we'll make it now."

Then after a moment she said with a sparkle in her eye, "On to Key West."

We passed Bahia Key hours later. "One more achievement," she said. Then, "Can we go all the way to the very end?"

"Yes. To the very end."

"I mean to the farthest land, right at the water's edge where we can't go anymore."

"Yes. We will go right to the end."

A few more miles rolled by. "I was always more a discoverer than your father."

"Yes. I know. You are a discoverer, Billie."

"But I couldn't ask for anyone better than your father. He was a good man."

"Yes he was, Billie. He was a good man. I mean, he is a good man."

Mother was becoming a renewed woman right before my eyes. And I was a grateful son, vicariously living her victory with her.

Finally, nearing Key West at mile marker fifteen, she said something important out of her deep thoughts.

"I wonder if your father is with us."

She looked at me, expecting an answer. Ever since my time on Zane Grey's mountain, I had been thinking about the ability of loved ones gone to know what is happening now on earth. I had been reading the Bible most of my life, but lately I'd been reading scriptures more closely, to find deeper answers, after Jeff died. Now I voiced my newly formed beliefs to her.

"I have an opinion about whether Dad is with us, Billie." She was still looking at me. "I do think Dad is here. I mean, God doesn't need to cut off such important things as family love when one dies. Why would He? God is love, and He knows you love Dad. He knows Dad loves you, and He loves both of you. He said everything else in the world would go away, but not love. He said that would never go away."

Billie didn't say anything. She was listening, drinking it in.

"I mean, I think love is love. It isn't one kind here and another kind there. We make up these other kinds of love down here on earth—like family love, married love, agape love. But how can there be more than one kind of love when God is love? Maybe we detract from love when we put adjectives in front of it."

I looked at her. "What do you think?"

"Love is okay, whatever it is," Billie said, reducing all my analysis to profound simplicity.

"Billie, you know it says in the Bible that we are encompassed about by a great cloud of witnesses?"

"Yes, I do."

"Dad could be one of them. I think he is here. He wouldn't be the first one to come back. You remember when Jesus went up on a high, lonely hill with Peter, James, and John, and two others came to talk with Him?"

With her years of Bible reading, Billie knew the story well, and her mind was alert.

"Those two creatures who came weren't angels," I said. "They were people. They were Moses and Elijah, who once lived here on earth. They knew what was happening here, and they returned and were talking with Jesus."

She thought awhile. "That's right. That's what happened."

When she said earlier, "I wonder if your father is here," she was voicing what many people secretly wonder when a loved one has gone. But our culture doesn't want to get into that. Perhaps because it sounds like some strange teachings of a cult. Perhaps because we've read that there are no more tears or sorrow in heaven, we can't imagine that those gone from earth could know what is going on here without sorrow. So by dismissing the possibility that the relationship with a loved one can still be an active one, we deprive ourselves of the comfort of continuing an ongoing love with those who are gone.

It never occurred to me that Billie might mistake my thoughts as some kind of seance theology. She didn't. "Love is okay," she said, so simply.

We were finally arriving in Key West, and I drove right down to the end of the island.

75

"Are we as far as we can go?"

"Yes. We could walk farther. But we've come as far as we can drive."

She smiled when I told her we would walk to the ocean later. Touring the town, she said, "I could live here."

Then we pulled up to a waterside hotel.

"You mean we're staying here?"

"Yes."

"Why? We don't need a hotel. I can sleep in the car. You can sleep in the front, and I can sleep in the back, and we'll save a lot of money."

It was a way of life she had learned in the twenties and thirties. Never eat in a restaurant; always take a picnic basket on a trip. Find the least expensive place to sleep, or sleep in the car. But go explore the world whether you have enough money or not.

"All my life I've always had to accommodate," she said. But now we checked in to excellent accommodations, a water-view room on the top floor.

We were ready to explore Key West. But within the hour the elevator broke down, the cable TV went out, even room service was late, and I couldn't get her down to the lobby in the wheelchair. But by now we were making a joke out of everything. "What more can go wrong?" we asked.

"Well," I said. "The food is pretty bad."

"But the water's good," she said, laughing.

"All the way to Key West, and everything is broken, and you say, 'The water is good.' You're a great lady, Billie."

We were having a marvelous time. Billie was thinking, remembering, laughing.

"You know, Billie, I think God is telling us something."

"I don't," she said, laughing. "If He is He has to tell us what."

And I thought, *How detailed is God's talk? How specific are His instructions?*

I knew I had received an unmistakable premonition about the specific timing of this trip. My client had moved a program we were to run, making more time for this trip together. And I had sensed that God was arranging this period of our lives for some special reason, although I didn't need to understand what it was.

I was just to be here with Billie, to be available and serve her just as I had learned to do with Jeff years before in his hospital isolation room, as I had done with Dad when I gave him a bath he was no longer able to give himself.

There is a great unwritten law. We understand *after* we obey, not before. And we do not always need to understand.

"Is tomorrow Sunday?" Billie asked.

"Yes. Tomorrow is Sunday." I was pleased that she was so aware of the calendar.

"Then if tomorrow is Sunday, we've got to go to church."

"What church do you want? There are several here."

"You pick the church, and I'll go with you."

So we attended a service in an all-white church building that had only black worshipers inside, except for us. The service was underway as I wheeled Billie in. People stole a glance, and when our eyes met, the fellow worshipers beamed beautiful smiles. It was a gracious place.

After the service had gone on for a long time, Billie needed to find a ladies' room. There was none in sight, so we left as quietly as we could. An attractive, full-bodied woman followed us out to the entry.

"You come back again, will you?"

"We're just vacationing, but we enjoyed your service."

"I'm glad you liked it. My husband and I come down from Miami every weekend to keep this church open. Fourteen years now."

Then she looked closely at Billie in her wheelchair, decked out in her old French-looking hat and her blue spring coat. She leaned down and said softly, "You're a very beautiful lady."

It was the same throughout our wheelchairing tour in and out of Key West throngs. People of all ages watched as I wheeled Billie by. Their eyes automatically rested on her, sizing her up, admiring the frail little body and the courage of her upright chin. Then they would look at me, saying whole paragraphs of approval with their smiles.

Once I stepped inside a small store that had a step too high to handily get Billie in. I left her outside the doorway momentarily as I checked something just inside the door. As always, her perky little hat and her bright blue coat and something indescribable about her attracted attention. A small group was standing nearby with wonder on their faces, then relief as I stepped outside the door and rejoined Billie.

While we strolled the dock, a young man in his thirties couldn't resist separating from the crowd and coming over to touch her shoulder. Bending over and smiling straight into her face he said, "You have a good day." Then he touched me on the shoulder, communicating a silent thanks.

I think that in a way he was saying something to his own mother, telling me of his gratitude as a fellow son.

I don't know how many people were helped just by seeing Billie out there on the docks, winding through the streets of Key West in her "chauffeured" wheelchair. As I watched the reactions I had the sense that it was a much bigger number of watchers than I'd have thought. And the reactions came from different folks.

One was a sausage vendor who watched her coughing, then walked over, thrusting something at me. Thinking it was an advertising leaflet, I was about to wave him away, then I saw he was handing me a thick roll of napkins. Surprised, I said, "Thank you," and he laughed, looking me in the eye, knowing what I had thought. "Have a good evening," he said in a sophisticated voice.

Another response came from a black teenager about junior-high-school age. He watched us wheeling toward him, then caught my eye and raised his fingers in a "V." He didn't need to say one word; nor did I, as I silently returned the sign. It was a simple, silent communication, a deep one that cut across the years and the races.

We are all sons and daughters. And in our practice of showing love we become brothers and sisters to others, even uncles or aunts to strangers we pass silently in the street.

We left Key West in high spirits and drove back up the Keys to Naples, to Sarasota, and finally to Tampa, allowing ourselves several days of adventure along the way. The important part of the adventure was seeing how little children noticed Billie. And how she noticed them. One little girl in a restaurant came up to our table and just stood there, smiling shyly at Billie. And Billie smiled back. Neither said a word. Nor did I, as I watched. Neither was saying anything, just unconsciously appreciating each other. It was a privileged moment to see the two of them, old and young, communicating without one word. I was watching the prompting of God.

We must capture these silent moments of life. There is so much going on in the silent times, so many opportunities to see the beauty of God in the little smiles of life.

Later, wheelchairing through Tampa airport before catching our flight to New York, I saw it happen again, but this time it was a one-way communication. A toddler was being pushed past us in a stroller while I pushed Billie the other way. Neither the child's parents nor Billie saw what I saw. The plump little boy couldn't take his eyes off my mother in her wheelchair. Turning in his stroller as he went by, he looked back, stretching to keep his eyes on her as long as he could.

We begin our years traveling in strollers and end them in wheelchairs, heading in different directions, and we look at each other on the way in wonder.

But Billie had amassed far more wisdom than the children she met. Considering that she didn't have the ability to determine the direction, timing, or course of our trip by herself, she employed considerable executive skill. She relied on three wise questions:

- Do you know where you are going?
- Do you know where you are?
- Does this motel room have two beds?

If I said yes to all three, she knew the day was all right, and she delegated the rest to me. She did it with a great sense of humor. At one point when she asked whether I knew where we were going I said, "Naples." And she replied, laughing, "This better not be Italy."

In Tampa when I asked her how she was she said, "Considering my age I'm pretty good, and that's what I'd better be today."

And when I remarked in the airport that we were about to take off she grinned and asked, "What are you taking off? I'm not taking anything off."

We are looking for little ways, you and I, to show our appreciation for our mothers, just as a little girl did who stood by at a restaurant table in shy friendship, and as a junior-high boy did with his silent "V" of approval, and a young sausage vendor did, too, as he offered what he had to help. And a young man in his thirties reached out, touched, and smiled his wish for mother, saying while looking into Billie's eyes, "You have a good day." We all need to stop and look into our mother's eyes and say, "You have a good day," because that is simple love at work.

The older people knew what was happening with Billie and me and showed it by their approving looks.

Someday it will be our turn. We are all on the same journey. And we all have a similar task, learning to listen to God's silent language.

I listened in Tampa Airport when Billie had the dry heaves for a while. "I'm sorry, Don," she said. "I hadn't planned on that." Nor had I planned on what would happen when we got home. Then I would need to listen even harder. To listen to a different message. To respond with a different form of obedience.

We flew home with anxiety. Billie must have worried about being sick, but she never said a word about it. The trip through Florida had sparked the old vitality in Billie, but the nausea in Tampa told me something else was wrong. Something new.

She rested quietly on the flight.

Our plane finally dropped down over the lights of New Jersey, veered over the edge of the dark Atlantic Ocean, crossed the huge Verrazano Bridge with its cables looped like a giant string of Christmas tree lights across the black Hudson River, flowing down from the Adirondacks and meeting the open sea at this precise spot. Now flying low along the length of Manhattan's canyons of dazzling lights, our plane banked right and floated softly down to the La Guardia runway, touched, and rumbled to a stop. None of this stirred Billie, not the lights, not the rumble of the wheels on the runway, not our darting through the surge of people coming and going through the passenger gates.

Wheeling her into the Admiral's Club, I didn't need to ask the attendants for help. They took one look, then cleared the ladies' room so I could wheel Billie in. Then Kevin met us with the car and we sped over the Whitestone Bridge, a question looming over me. Can we make it home without a major illness? A stop, a dry heave, and on again.

Back home in Pound Ridge, we put Billie to bed, but she grew worse over the next two days. I had to leave town, and while I was gone Joan admitted her to nearby Greenwich Hospital. I came back and took my turn sleeping overnight at her bedside. I remembered the night spent with Jeff in his hospital isolation room years before, and I prayed, "Lord, you know. . . ."

Slowly Billie improved. The doctor came into the room one day with an air of confidence. "She became toxic due to an overdose of medicine. We can clean that up in a few days and she can go home."

My attention to her exact dosage of medicine had been too precise. When Billie was alone in Long Lake she forgot to take her medicine just enough times to make the dosage right. But when I took over during our trip, I made sure she took the exact prescription, by then too much for her.

Finally detoxified and returning to our home in Pound Ridge, Billie was at her peak. The doctors had said, prophetically, "Your mother will probably never be in better health for the rest of her life." But her memory had not improved, making a return to the cold winters in Long Lake unthinkable to me. Two sisters had stayed overnight at the hospital, and both shared our family joy at Billie's return. Now both were standing by in eager expectation, hoping for the opportunity to take Billie home with them. I had decided to support Vangie, who could watch over mother constantly. But Esther, hoping mother would return to Long Lake, maintained that she could provide the better care.

When it becomes clear that there is little time left for your last parent to be with you, the children sometimes struggle over who should provide the care. And other struggles from earlier years that long ago seemed resolved or were never recognized now rise to consciousness. It is a time of vague fears, intense feelings, growing awareness, and finally honest debate. The issue of who is right gets in the way of what is right.

Our three-way polite veneer cracked, then broke wide open into real disagreement the next day, while Billie was present.

"I'll be taking mother home now, to Long Lake."

"Mother has just returned from the hospital. She isn't ready to go anywhere right now."

"But she belongs in Long Lake."

"She belongs where she can be cared for."

It was now an open battle between my older sister and me, both feeling we were right. Then in her sweet spirit Vangie said quietly, "It will be a privilege for Harold and I to have a turn to care for mother in our home." That was seven hours away, out near Buffalo.

Billie, still the mother, broke in, worried and wise in her new strength. "I'm surprised at all this," she said. "I want each of you to settle down. I want you to find a way to agree."

It was as though someone had torn off years from our life calendars. It was as though Billie were forty and we were all children again. Maybe we were. We listened to her. Billie had said nothing of her wish for herself, just of her wish for her three grown-up children groping their way through the age-old question: Who will take care of mother?

There is a leftover child in all of us when the last parent has a short time left and a warning of death has come so close.

So we finally agreed to disagree on the way to care for Billie. We had not yet begun to ask ourselves an important guiding question, "What's good for mother?"

But the tension wouldn't go away. It hung over everyone like some sick presence that was infecting all of us with a disease we couldn't see. I feared for the effect on Billie.

In a room where Billie couldn't overhear I said to Esther, "I think it will be better for Billie if you leave."

It was a shock. Stunned silence hung in the room. Nothing like that had happened before in our family.

"If I go I will never come back here again," she said. She went in to mother's chair in the next room, spent some time with her, and left.

Billie cried. Cheerful, vivacious, wise, loving Billie cried.

Later that night the blessing of memory loss allowed Billie to engage in a bright, witty, and joyful conversation. She had not been so spontaneous for years, and when she went to bed all was well.

Until early next morning. Vangie knocked on our bedroom door.

"Donnie." She used my nickname from childhood days. "Something is wrong with mother."

Racing in to Billie's bedroom, Joan and I found Billie unable to speak, pointing to her head, making a soft noise.

"Call Greenwich Hospital and tell them we're on the way to the emergency room," I said. In minutes Vangie and I were on the way with Billie, trying to reassure her. "We're only ten minutes away now, Billie. . . . Only five now. . . . You're going to be all right. . . . Two minutes now, Billie." The car was racing but our voices were measured and slow, and Billie said nothing. She couldn't speak another word.

The emergency room was ready. They hooked up the instruments, read the fearful news, asked us to wait outside. After moments that seemed like hours the doctor finally came out.

"She has suffered a stroke. It's a big one. We'll need to get her admitted right away."

We rode with Billie to the same floor she had just left two days ago. The same doctors and nurses hovered over her, knowing who she was, remembering her departing smile.

Bill Hillis, the chief surgeon, came by as a friend. "Let me know what you want me to do. I'm here."

We were in the best place possible for Billie. Now it wasn't a question of Long Lake or Pound Ridge or the Buffalo area. It was Greenwich Hospital, with the best room, the best staff, the best accommodations we could find. Billie was on the hospice floor, with access to a library, a spacious living room, a guest room, and the wisdom of years of hospice training. Even better, this was Joan's territory. Since her ordination, she had served as associate pastor at Stanwich Congregational Church in Greenwich. She visited this hospital often in her ministerial capacity. Soon everyone was there to help. Vangie had never left. Now Marilyn came, with all her warmth and insight and her busy schedule resolved. And Esther returned.

It was a time for all of us to listen to God's silent language, to strain for the meaning in this new illness. There were no words from mother. But there were plenty of words from the doctors.

Three of them came to the same conclusion. Massive stroke. No recovery. Just a matter of time.

But I had to know something. I asked all three doctors, to be sure I understood. "Could we have caused the stroke, doctor? We . . . we had an argument between the members of the family about where mother would live. And it wasn't a polite argument. There were deep feelings, and they all spilled out . . . and mother was there. Could we have. . . ?"

"No. Whatever you said, it couldn't have altered the course of your mother's stroke. She was on a collision course with this stroke for many years. Even if you could have altered the time, it would have been only a day or so. You see, this is a big stroke. Your mother is living, but she's not really alive."

Now we had to talk about the ultimate question, and it had become painfully clear that we must answer it. What do we do about how long mother "lives"? We four, three daughters and one son, hold the destiny of our mother in our decision. But how do we individually come to know what is right? How do we hear God's message? And how can we possibly agree?

If we remove all life-saving instruments, are we snuffing out Billie's life? If we leave them hooked up, are we merely continuing the suffering? Do we have the right to turn them off? And did we have a right to hook them up in the first place, especially when Dad and Billie had always said they didn't want them? What does the law say? Does New York law or Connecticut law apply? What does "the law" know about Billie anyway?

Nothing.

So we slowly returned to the basic questions of life. What does God know about Billie? Everything. But is He going to tell us?

No. Not in words. Only in His silent language.

And so gradually, as we continued to examine our souls and talk with one another, the steadying question emerged: "What's good for Billie?" If Billie were deciding, what would Billie decide?

"I want to stay right here, as your father did," she had said. "I go out on my porch swing at the end of the day and watch the sun light up a path of diamonds across the water to the shore."

I checked with the hospital's administrative staff. "We let the family decide what's right," they said. "We aren't bound by any law in these cases."

This came as a relief to each of us. In these days of complicated legality, we still can do what's best for Billie! So in a few days we moved her into the hospice unit. Her room had flowered wallpaper, an adjoining guest room, beautiful wood furniture, and a window with a view of the sunset. You could see Long Island Sound to the left of her window, and lying on the horizon was distant New York City, its blinking lights barely visible. It was as close as we could get to Long Lake. But Billie couldn't see any of it.

I looked out the window at a sunset waning behind heavy clouds. It slowly faded away to darkness, and the darkness revealed the faraway lights of New York, winking like diamonds.

Here I am, I thought, *waiting for mother to leave. And there on the horizon is the city where I stood a few years ago over Jeff, waiting, listening, as I am now.* Then I remembered the Presence and knew I was not alone here in Greenwich.

When Vangie and I were together a few days later and the nurse came in, I said, "Please . . . cut that off." I pointed to the intravenous tube. I don't know if mother heard me, but we all recognized somehow that Billie wanted to go home. The nurse had told us earlier, with compassion in her voice, "You don't need to make her endure this suffering, you know."

What's good for mother? It was no longer a question, but a way to discern and to arrive at agreement.

When Marilyn had left earlier she said with wisdom and tenderness, her soft voice barely breaking the stillness, "Rest sweetly, little Mamma." It was one of those special moments to hear, to feel. Esther, too, was at peace about mother's leaving. She said, "Mother wants to go home," and now she was not talking about Long Lake. Now as we were leaving the room, Vangie, who had wanted so much to have the privilege of serving mother in her own home, leaned over and kissed her and watched Billie die without a word, without a move.

"Goodbye, my sweet little mother," she said.

Goodbye, Billie. Goodbye, exploring companion. And say hello for me, Billie. Hello, bright new land. Hello, Dad. Hello, Jeff.

Silence. Billie had gone home.

Charming Billie. Everybody wants to see you, Billie. A little girl standing by your table in a Florida restaurant. A pudgy little boy in a stroller couldn't keep his eyes off you. A junior-high boy sitting on a curb making a "V" sign saw you, Billie. A young man was bending over you saying, "You have a good day." You aren't just some eighty-nine-year-old lady who can't smile anymore. You're Billie, do you hear? Billie. You hear me, Billie? I love you, Billie. So . . . you are home, my sweet little Billie.

But I was not home yet. I still had other journeys to make.

Part Three

New Windows,
New Voices

7

THE VIEW FROM THE TRAIN

A CROSS-COUNTRY PILGRIMAGE

"For the windows of heaven are opened."

—The Book of Isaiah

Episode I: The Silence of Glaciers

Joan and I knew something was wrong. I had suddenly become stalled in life, unable to focus or move forward, certainly unable to hear God's voice or to sense His presence. I had no name for my feeling and no prescription for changing it, only the suspicion that a long train ride would help.

I remembered the special vision on the train years ago, after Jeff died. My train passed Manhattan's parade of buildings and I saw the spiritual shadow of my father's Adirondack Mountains superimposed in that moving train window. I felt the silent message of the Lord there. For me, since then, trains have become a special place for quiet time—a time to understand, a time to hear God, and to write about what I think and see. Now I desperately needed such a place again. All the perspective I had been granted after Dad's and Jeff's deaths seemed to have vanished, along with my sense of who I was and where I was heading.

This was nothing a walk in the country or a weekend in a nice hotel would cure. So I put my business on hold and booked a berth on Amtrak. I would ride the rails from New York to Chicago, from Glacier Mountain Park in Montana to Portland, Oregon, then down the West Coast to Los Angeles, across Arizona and New Mexico to Texas and points east. After a few days of rest on the shores of Mobile Bay in Alabama, I would complete the circle—up through Atlanta, Washington, Philadelphia, and finally New York again.

Joan couldn't go with me this time. Her church responsibilities called her to remain in Connecticut. Besides, a trip we made from Helsinki to Leningrad to Moscow had permanently quenched her thirst for rail travel. "I've had all the train rides I need for the rest of my life, thank you," she said.

But for me this trip wasn't simply a train ride. This was a quest for new discernment and vitality. I needed to step back from my everyday life long enough to get a new perspective. I needed to hear the silent voice I had lost. I needed to write what I heard, to get what was inside me out where I could understand it.

For weeks, the process of planning my trip had given me a fresh sense of anticipation. But now as Joan and I rushed to the commuter station in suburban Mt. Kisco, I found it hard to leave. "I may call you partway around the country and tell you I'm flying home."

"You're having second thoughts?"

Her question was tentative. She didn't want me to go.

"I'm going to miss you," she said, looking at the road ahead.

"Me, too," I replied, feeling it already. We pulled into the train station. It was a little like leaving her at the Schenectady train station during the Korean War. Then we discovered that we could overcome everything, but it was so hard. Joan and I looked at each other in the car, trading lonesome smiles. "You take care of yourself."

"I will. I'll call you whenever I can. But I'll be on the train most of the time, you know."

"I know, and you can have it," she said, trying to be cheerful.

I hesitated. "Joan . . . I've got to do this. I don't know why. I can't seem to get anything done. I've . . . lost something." I looked over at her. "I need to find a way to get things rolling again."

She was quiet for a while. "I'll miss you," she finally repeated.

Then she looked at her watch. "The train's due any minute now. We'd better hurry."

I raced for the platform at commuter speed, making it with two minutes to spare. Pulling into New York City fifty minutes later, I had to race the clock again. My train arrived late in Grand Central and I had only half an hour to cab across town to catch the Broadway Limited for Chicago. I spotted the roof light on an empty yellow taxi.

"Can you make it to Penn Station by ten of two?" I asked the driver.

He blew air out of his nose in a reverse sniff. "It's twenty-three of two now!" he said. But he made it.

Inside Penn station everything slowed down! The Broadway Limited was an hour late. But when we finally got started we really rolled, first heading south to Philadelphia, then nosing west toward Chicago, and I settled in to enjoy the clean green beauty of the peaceful Amish and Mennonite farms that rolled by my window. After riding into the golden sunset in the dining car, I climbed into my roomette bunk and slept my rumbling way toward the great metropolis of the Midwest.

After a good long walk around friendly Chicago during the middle of the next day, I boarded the Empire Builder for the next leg of my journey. We traveled north through St. Paul. Then we swung left, picking up speed for the straight run west along the thousand-mile Great Northern route.

Crossing the Great Plains with hardly a curve for an afternoon and a night and another full day makes you appreciate the awe-inspiring achievement of taming the great northern plains. Only as I finally began to see the northern Rocky Mountains did I feel a sense of extraordinary anticipation. The Empire Builder, now late enough to meet a rarely timed full-color sunset over the Rockies, rolled across the plains while I enjoyed a late dinner in the dining car. I watched the color silently move from cloud to cloud across the vast sky. Then, just before we reached the mountains, the land outside my window began to rise and fall, the once-flat plains rolling by in slow waves. We passed rising brown buttes and waning green valleys. And then I saw the Rockies, sharply sweeping up from the earth like some ancient monuments, their stillness startled by the sleek double-level superliner whistling its long-last arrival at the long log train station at Glacier National Park.

"We're always drawn back to this place," said Bob Hawkes, a fellow traveler. He talked to me about the Glaciers as we were racing across the plains. "It's the silence," he said. "There's something healing in the silence of the place."

I realized when he said it. *That's just what I need.* I wanted the healing of the silence, though I hadn't even known I was sick.

Bob and Betsy Hawkes and I met on the train as it hurtled across the vast plains toward the silent mountains. We chatted about where we were from and where we were going. And gradually we became friends, as our trust grew.

After a while I lent Bob a copy of my little book *Fatherbond*, the one I wrote after Jeff died. He returned it two hours later. "I want to talk with you," he said.

We went to my compartment and we talked a long time about fathers and sons, about what it means to be a father and a son. Men don't find many opportunities to talk so openly with other men. So it was a good time for us, talking about such significant things while the Empire Builder rolled on toward the still mountains.

The impact of a father on a son molds the way the son lives his life with his own family and the way he approaches a career. It must be the same for mothers and daughters. All of us tend to live the way we have seen life lived by our parents when we were young. Or we write ourselves an emotional prescription that we will never treat our children the way we were treated. But sooner or later we do it anyway, until something happens to change us in a powerful way. Something like the death of a son.

As my father grew older, I became more and more aware of his legacy of strength, discipline, and faith. I could see that he loved me. But he showed his love indirectly, as fathers did in those days, giving advice and listening and wanting to know how I was doing as I got older. But I was ready for more expression. That is why I took the initiative and began to hug my father.

The first Christmas of the experiment I waited until we were about to leave my parents' house. I stood in front of him. "Dad," I said, not wanting to risk a misunderstanding, "I'm going to do something that may seem a little odd. I understand some fathers and sons give each other a hug as a way to show that they love each other. So I'm going to give you a hug," I said. "And I'm going to tell you that I love you." Sometimes you need to prepare someone you love for a new way, to show that you really care.

He stood in wonder as I gave him the first hug I can remember. He didn't return it, nor did he say anything. I said, "I love you, Dad," and then I left.

The next Christmas I tried again. "Remember last year when I gave you a hug, Dad? I'm going to do that again and tell you that I love you." I gave him a bear hug for the second time in my life and I said, "I love you, Dad." He still didn't return the hug, and he didn't say, "I love you." But this time he was relaxed. He wasn't the statue he was the first time.

It was the third Christmas, when I said again as I was leaving, "Remember the last two years when I said I love you and I gave you a hug? I'm going to do that again."

I stepped in front of him, as he stood, taller than me, and I gave him a strong bear hug. "I love you, Dad," I said. And this time he returned my hug with a more powerful one! He was stronger than a bear. "I love you, son," he said, looking at me.

My "hugging lessons" with Dad were important for him. But they were even more important for me, and for my children. If something is worth doing, it is worth doing with the patient understanding that change takes time. And even if the other person never changes, you have changed. That is the important thing.

The delay of our train made it impossible for me to make it to the hotel I had booked for the night, and Betsy was concerned. "The owner of our motel is picking us up," she said. "You can ride with us and maybe find a motel." When she found there were no more rooms in their motel, she asked, "Can you put a cot in our room for him?" But the driver said he didn't have any extra cots.

He drove to a huge hotel right next to the station. "Try here," he said. "Sometimes they have an extra room for someone who arrives on the train."

I stepped into the lobby of the handsome old Glacier Mountain Lodge, built by the Great Northern Railroad before 1920 out of huge northwestern logs. I asked for a room, and the young clerk said, "Sorry." Then, "Wait, there's one room left. It's not our best, but you can have it if you want it." Gratefully I climbed to the third-floor room and settled into bed, deciding that the next day I would follow one of Bob and Betsy Hawkes' favorite trails to mountain silence. To healing.

"Many Glacier" is an old name for a place of rare beauty, high in the mountains. The old Many Glacier Hotel is even more spectacular than Glacier Mountain Lodge, where I had stayed. The great grizzly bear makes his home in the high country surrounding this hotel. A trail hike requires you to make a lot of noise to let the grizzlies know you are coming, to give them time to clear out. They become more grizzly when they are taken by surprise.

Hiking five miles up and around the mountains to secluded Iceberg Lake, I encountered some of the most striking scenery in America—a range of intimate spring flowers at my feet, a convoy of mountain goats moving slowly across a high mass of snow to a new spring patch of grass. Even an occasional snow mass, drifted deep across my trail. When I crossed the snow single file with the other climbers, I realized that one slip could send me sliding down the mountain until I reached a row of trees far below, or a sheer precipice that I couldn't even see. That stark realization made me carefully plant my steps in the melting snow, each step freezing my thoughts.

Finally, safely across the snow mass, the line of hikers swept slowly left around the last mountain to catch the first glimpse of a lake that must have existed for thousands of years. I hiked down to the water's edge. On the opposite shore, facing me, rose a fifteen-hundred-foot sheer rock wall. Sometimes snow masses roar down the side and plunge into the lake with a dull, thundering sound, making a great wave that finally washes to shore. The water was clear, sparkling, inviting to a hiker with hot, tired feet. Quickly I stripped off socks and boots and dipped my bare feet. Four quick steps and I was back out. The stabbing cold of the high wilderness water spoke to me in a clear, silent command: "Get out of here."

By the time I reached Iceberg Lake I had become acquainted with two or three fellow hikers. We had clustered on the trail in mutual fear of the grizzly bears. So on the way back down I stayed with them. Two from San Francisco, two from New York, and two from Australia seemed pleased by the company. I needed them and they needed me, if for no other reason than the additional noise we made.

Fearful trips make traveling companions of people who might never speak to one another in safer circumstances. It works the same way in our walk with God. We edge closer when we are afraid.

Down from the high trail, sweaty from the long hike back to the relative warmth of the valley, I gladly paid one dollar for a token at a campground shower and fifty cents for a small bar of soap. Stripping in haste and about to plug in the token for eight minutes' worth of hot water, I realized I had no towel. *Paper towels will do fine*, I thought, proud of my ingenuity as I plugged in the token and revelled in the burst of hot water that splashed deliciously over me. "Eight minutes is plenty of time," I said to myself, rinsing down and lathering my hair a second time. At this moment the hot water shut off, leaving me with soap suds dripping down my back.

The camp store with the tokens was more than yelling distance away, and there was not a soul in the shower area. I thought quickly, *Out there in the entry at the washbasin is plenty of hot water and more paper towels. If I can only dash there and back before some kid comes in and accuses me of indecent exposure. . . ."*

Peeking out into the stillness I chanced it. I dashed to the sink and cupped handfuls of hot water over my hair, under my arms, and down my naked presence. I had never rinsed faster and seldom prayed more quickly.

Back in the shower stall with a handful of paper towels, I started blotting. And at that moment, in came a camper to the shower area. Timing is everything.

I was laughing by now, glowing with the exercise, revitalized by the water, chuckling at life. Something was happening already. Almost without realizing it, I was becoming renewed.

Episode II: To a Pacific View

It is an experience to stand at the edge of the ancient Rocky mountains at an old train station that divides the Great Plains from the massive mountains and to see a sleek new superliner gliding in from modern Chicago. East meets west and old meets new. And that's where I met three people who were so good-natured and genuine that we became platform friends in the few moments before the train arrived.

I was later to see that our meeting on the platform and our ride together was no coincidence, as fewer things seem to me now. Ed and Gerry, husband and wife, had decided to vacation with Marge, Gerry's sister. Now they were on their way back to California after a vacation by train around the Midwest.

There was a presence among these three. A sense of beliefs strongly held but not spoken. They were having a good time and showing a spirit of congenial thanksgiving for their trip.

I said to Marge, "You are showing a warm spiritual presence."

"Thank you," she said, looking at me. "Where are you heading?"

"I'm writing my way around the country. I'm writing the rest of a book I wrote a few years ago about my father and son who both died of cancer." She looked at me more closely now.

"You will be a success in what you write because you have been successful in the way you have dealt with that."

I was surprised by the note of commitment in her words. She didn't say, "I hope you will be a success," which would have been a nice thing to say, but one of those superficial comments that pass through our consciousness without making a difference.

Most of what people say to us—and what we say to others—lacks such commitment; that's why it is usually discounted by the listener. And words that do carry commitment are too often coercive—spoken to control or change others. These are usually deflected by the shields of our defenses. But when we speak with commitment in our words yet without trying to change others, we make a spiritual connection, whether or not the person knows it at the time. This silent language lives within the language we speak and is the thing that really causes people to listen.

If we are patient, if we listen carefully and don't give up, we can learn to sense the spirit behind the words people use. This listening beyond the words is the equivalent of patiently seeking the glacial silence.

We boarded the packed train and found our separate seats, but met again in the dining car for the evening meal. As the train wound its way through the Rockies, we ate and watched a red sun settling down behind the enormous mountain peaks into darkness.

Few restaurants in the world match the view of this one.

By the time our train had broken through the mountain pass, raced on to Spokane through the night, and followed the course of the mighty Columbia River down to Portland, we had established an unspoken agreement to eat each meal together.

We reached the relaxed city of Portland with a few hours to spare before we had to catch the Coast Starlight train south, so we agreed to share a cab to the city's International Rose Garden. We spent most of that sunny Sunday afternoon walking through rose beds. Fields of rosebushes in shades of color I had never seen spread around us like fragrant quilts. From the strings of two musicians, in perfect harmony, came the sounds of Vienna, Rome, Paris. Strolling off to the side, hearing the music rise up behind, I found myself drawn to a single small bloom, its petals delicately furled around a miniature golden heart.

After soaring peaks and vast glacier fields I responded to this intimate beauty of tiny rose petals, the soft humming of bees—a faint voice from a violin. I realized anew what I had begun to understand from the hospital maintenance man years before. If we focus carefully enough, we really can begin to hear God, to notice the language of the Lord in everything around us, from immeasurable cliffs to miniature rose petals—to the soul of another human, creating compelling sounds of music in a field of a million roses. We aren't promised a rose garden, but we can find it, if we look, if we stop to recognize it once we're there.

We boarded the Coast Starlight train again and headed down the length of Oregon, laboring our way up over the Cascade Mountains, gliding through stately stands of evergreen.

My dad would have been captivated by those cool forests. He was a husbandman of the woods as well as a man of God, able to preach a thoughtful sermon on Sunday and then on Monday drop a dying tree with his axe, cutting it to fall precisely between two young trees so as not to hurt them. I once came upon him as he prayed alone among the trees—the ones he had felled before his feet and the others standing tall above him as though looking on. His communion with God was partly as a caretaker of God's forest. His special unspoken communication was one of his many unknowing gifts to me—even more important than his Sunday sermons.

We threaded our way through the lakes and streams around Klamath Falls, Oregon, and then raced down from the soaring heights of northern California toward the sea level San Francisco-Oakland station, where Ed, Gerry, and Marge were scheduled to leave the train and go home. Our traveling party was speeding to a close.

The night before our train rolled into San Francisco, we all got together in my compartment. Packed into a little compartment designed for two, the four of us talked more intimately than we had up to then. We spoke about the deep feelings we all have in life.

Ed, an attorney, spoke of anger. "I've decided that other people don't have the power to make me angry. I'm the only one who can do that. Either I let myself become angry, or I become the master of anger."

Gerry explained her appreciation for honesty. "I really think it helps our relationships."

Marge's eyes filled with tears when we talked of losing a loved one. Her loss had been a painful divorce. "But I've gotten stronger," she said softly. "I've grown."

Now the four of us decided to end our day with a prayer. Open prayer might have seemed a risk earlier, when we were still strangers, but now it turned out to be no risk at all. Crammed tight, jostled gently by the train's motion, we were more like one than four as we each said our simple thanks for the scenes through our moving windows, for the friendships we had found. Then Marge quoted some beautiful words she had written in difficult years past. They were so helpful that I asked her to write them down for me. They became a new benediction to a day of watching the language of God in the glorious scenery—of hearing it above the low rumbling of a sleeping car as we pierced the night darkness at high speed, probing our way down the Pacific Northwest coast. Before going to sleep, I read her words again.

"The wind is the breath of God," I read. "The sun is the smile of God. The stars are the eyes of God. The rain is the tears of God. And children are the heart of God."

Good friends, even new friends, can speak and write with the voice of God, in the silent language of love and sharing.

Episode III: To Big Bend's Ancient Window

Alone in my compartment, racing farther down the California coast on the Coast Starlight train, I glided along the cliffs above the Pacific for more than a hundred miles. People looked up from their beach play to watch our train sweep by. There is something exciting about a train going by. It isn't just the train. People searched the moving windows and waved at the passengers. When we have the time, it's our natural inclination to wave at someone going somewhere, and there is a natural inclination to wave back to those who risk a wave.

In Los Angeles at dinnertime, I had a few hours between trains. I stepped out to the street to ask for directions to some restaurant that would give me a quiet interlude.

"Where can I go to get something decent to eat—someplace a little different?"

The security guard looked at me. "See that man talking with the police officer?"

"Yes."

"That man walked across the street a few minutes ago to get something to eat, right over there, and he was just beaten and robbed."

I didn't want to be that different. I thought of a conversation I had with Joan before leaving home. "Don't get mugged," she had cautioned, thinking of several near-misses on previous trips. This time I was just one person away from getting mugged again. I accepted my deliverance thankfully and ate a second-rate cafeteria meal in the station before boarding the famous Sunset Limited for Texas. Sometimes you select a second-rate meal in return for the opportunity to enjoy another meal later.

We sped across the Southwest desert for a night and a day and an evening, the hours broken by an occasional view of the ancient formations in the distance. I saw an extinct volcano in the distance. It had once spread boiling lava miles across the desert in a massive paving of the sand, up near to the route of my train. Separated from the volcano by several hours was an abandoned frontier village. The vast, still landscape punctuated occasionally by civilization—first vibrant Phoenix, then relaxed Tucson, and finally, many hours later, old El Paso. The vastness took over again and again until the train finally rumbled to a stop at 10:14 at night in sleepy little Alpine, Texas.

A quick call to the local airport manager, whom I knew had three used cars for rent, and in five minutes an old Lincoln Towncar pulled up to the lonely station. After quickly signing the rental papers, I speeded due south across the black desert toward Big Bend National Park. I had reservations in the park lodge, nestled high in the Chisos Mountains, a short drive from the Mexican border.

The next day, after a long sleep in a clean room high in the cool mountain night, I set out to explore the beauty of Big Bend. I looked out the window at a strikingly clear day. I couldn't see a cloud anywhere, just the light blue sky and the jagged peaks above me.

"Be sure and check out the sunset through the Window," the attendant at the lodge told me as I stepped toward the door for my first hike. "It's one of the things the park is famous for."

So that evening, sitting in ancient Chisos basin at a cool 5,400 feet above the still-baking Texas desert, I waited with a few other tourists for the sun to go down. Behind us towered craggy mountains that rise nearly eight thousand feet around a high plain created by a volcano millions of years ago. The sun has been going down here every day for at least that long. And I knew it was going to do it again in just a few minutes.

After weeks of looking through moving train windows, I was now ready to see the sun set through a massive window that hasn't moved for ages. Texans call it a window because two of the mountains that ring the basin don't quite make it around. The result is a high "V" that frames the sunset spectacularly. Every night people come here to see the beauty of the desert sunset from an ancient volcano seat.

"It will be beautiful tonight if there are clouds," the lodge attendant had commented before I left to take in the show.

"Yes," I said, "And that's the way it is in life. The clouds make us see the extra beauty beyond."

"You're right," she said, appearing to think it over.

Tonight's sunset promises to be a real event, judging by the lively way the wind is announcing it. At first there is only a pleasant breeze, refreshingly different from the 115-degree heat of the desert far below. The wind gusts momentarily, drawing our attention away from the majesty of changing color slowly forming in the sky beyond the big window. The wind suddenly sweeps around the massive basin, exercising the trees nearby, yet making no impact on the cliffs above.

This whistling wind commands our attention now, much as a trumpet blast at the precise point the communion host is raised in a great cathedral. It says: An important event is taking place in a moment. You can't simply see this sunset; you must listen as well as look. *You must feel the sunset here.*

Two dark mountains form the jagged frame of the window, the rocky heights bowing gradually to the sun at just the right point so that you see the distant sweep of the desert hills. The sun slides slowly down toward a massive cloud barely noticed before. Sneaking behind it, the sun lights up the edges of the cloud, highlighting its massive size and dwarfing the mountains I had watched all evening in awe.

Before my father died he said, "When I leave life I'm going to see if I can travel around the earth and see all of this creation from a different viewpoint. I'm going to see it all from the other side."

So, while I sit here remembering, looking through this window at the soft light of the heavens beyond, the darkening mountains in sharp relief against the light behind, I imagine angels sitting on those majestic clouds, looking through this placid earth-window from the other side, enjoying the look on my face. *Are you there, Dad?*

The hurried human seekers of instant sunsets who gathered moments ago have left now, thinking it's all over, and I am alone, still waiting for the mellowing color that may yet appear. In a moment a long pink ray slowly lights up the sky where there is no cloud. *How did that happen?* I think to myself. It lights up the clouds over the highest mountaintop, then slowly fades away, giving place to the purpling darkness behind as though on cue from a silent stage manager. Now the moon slides silently into view, announcing the end of the show. The wind whips its way down the canyon, calling back a hollow-sounding goodbye, and in the sudden stillness of the evening an awakened cricket voices its welcome to the dark. But I linger and say to whoever may be listening from the other side of the clouds, "Good-night, Great Father. Good-night, strong Dad. Good-night, sweet Billie. Good-night, my son."

It is good to practice noticing more than seems to be there at first glance. I find that creative noticing calls for patience, a commodity in short supply. The reward is a new perspective of earth through a willingness to consider the seeming one-way mirrors of life as two-way mirrors, which they are.

If you do this patient imagining right, the imagination that comes is not yours. It is the silent gift from another Presence, enjoying your face in the bright sun while you enjoy watching His creation. Creative thoughts come, seemingly from nowhere, just as the wind starts from nowhere and touches your brow with a new thought. One minute your mind is bound by measured thinking, and the next minute an immeasurable thought appears from nothing. To capture such creative thoughts we must put away our limited ideas so a new illuminating message can get through. We need to sense our creative heart as much as we sense our analytical head. Sometimes we must get "out of our minds" and let the real Creator speak to us. That is what I was practicing as I looked out God's window at Chisos Basin.

And the next day I practiced again. Heading up Lost Mine Trail with a jug of water, some trail mix, and some fruit, I felt the same quick burst of wind as I climbed higher and higher. I chose to interpret this wind as an encourager in the heat of the day. Some might have said, "It's just a wind. Everybody feels the same wind." But I was practicing the skill of listening for God's silent message in the wind as in everything else. All the way up the switchback trail I practiced by recognizing the Personality behind the beauty that confronted me at every turn.

When I finally reached the dizzying top of the narrow trail, I sat down and ate. Then, after all the thinking practice on my climb up the mountain, I wanted to capture some of my thoughts on paper. So I relaxed on the rounded peak and wrote, without knowing what I wanted to say. But when I wrote it, I knew. As I was writing, the thoughts seemed to appear at the end of the pen before they came to mind. By the time I made my contented way down the mountain, my paper was filled with thoughts I could not have recognized before.

I realized that when I *think* I have something to say I must say it or write it. Then, surprisingly, what I intend to say often becomes something else in the forming of the words. Through this mystery, I have heard God insert His language into my own words.

Down from Lost Mine Trail now, I packed my suitcase and spent a whole day driving through the baking desert on the way to the Rio Grande, the mighty river that marks off the border between Texas and Mexico. There it lay, at the end of a dry dirt road—the Rio Grande and, eighty feet farther, Mexico. I saw a man on the other side raise his arm and wave, saying something in Spanish.

I waved and pointed to myself and to him. Another unintelligible sentence came across the water. I waited as he talked to someone else over the bank. In a few minutes a young boy came over the bank, jumped down to an old rowboat and started paddling over the muddy river. I noticed how swift the current was and how he conquered it. He paddled upstream in the eddy, turned and faced the current, then paddled straight into it, letting his sideways force and the direct current bring the boat slanting across to the eddy on my side of the river just below where I was standing. When he touched the eddy on my side, he turned upstream again in the quiet water and paddled leisurely to my shore, now looking surprisingly small and young, whistling a soft tune.

"How much?" I asked.

"Two dollars," he answered with only a slight accent.

I hesitated.

"Round trip," he added. He was a discerning salesman.

Into the boat I climbed, then watched him use the eddy and the current again to land me on the Mexican bank.

"The town?" I asked.

He pointed over the bank. I climbed the path over the bank and walked the dusty stretch between stucco houses in a poor desert town. A radio blared a spicy mix of guitars, trumpets, accordions, and Spanish voices out into the blazing July heat. I spotted a dusty restaurant, just a converted living room of a house, and ordered a cold soft drink.

"Orange, Sprite, or Coke?" the young girl asked.

"Orange," I said, then added, "In the bottle." I had learned about Mexico before.

She left through a curtained exit to the kitchen. Waiting, I noticed the well-known picture on the wall of a man praying over a Bible, a loaf of bread, and a cup. The words above the picture said, "El pan nuestro de cada dia danosle hoy." Even without knowing Spanish, I understood: "Give us this day our daily bread."

The Mexican boat boy paddled me back across the Rio Grande, whistling his way contentedly. The whistling told the story. Here is a boy who doesn't fight the river. He uses it. And I was learning a lesson here. If you want to get across an impossible river that keeps you from your destination in life, you don't try to paddle straight across. Instead, you conserve your energy, use your head, paddle upstream in the quiet waters and use the current to carry you across. Then a few strokes of your paddle at the right moment will carry you to the next eddy on the other side. It still takes effort, but it's far easier than a frontal assault. And if you remember that a young boy can do it, you too can whistle while you work your way across.

Safely ashore in Texas, I knew it had come time for me to cross the desert for the one-hundred-mile race to meet the Sunset Limited, speeding its way at that moment from Los Angeles toward the little town of Alpine, where it stopped only three times a week at 10:14 P.M. Now I was in a hurry. If I didn't make that train, I would be stuck in that sleepy West Texas town for a few more nights, and I didn't need that much sleep!

Episode IV: Silent Supertrain to San Antonio

When I rolled into Alpine, the train station was locked. There wasn't a person on the street. I meandered through town slowly in my old rented Lincoln, passing a few restaurants and finally stopping at the Sunday Inn. I asked myself silently, *Is this the right place?* and took another sweep up the street. Giving in finally to my first inclination, I turned back to the motel and walked in.

It was the right place. But you couldn't tell right away.

The first room the waitress led me to was dark, smoky, and jammed full of Texans enjoying a Chinese buffet. Definitely the in place to eat in Alpine, but I couldn't tell why. It occurred to me that perhaps a Chinese buffet in a dark room in a desert town wasn't a smart idea. What were they trying to hide? Besides, I couldn't see a Chinese person anywhere. So I declined the buffet, and the waitress directed me back to the same room I had first entered. It was brighter, more Texan, so I ordered fajitas, figuring they were a better bet than egg rolls in a West Texas town.

Then, a moment later, it became startlingly apparent why I was not only in the right place but in the right room at the right moment.

Behind me, the waitress asked a man whether the train would be late.

"Yep. It's really late this time."

"What time'll it be here?"

"Six-thirty tomorra mornin'."

I couldn't resist joining the conversation. It had to be my train they were discussing.

"Are you serious?" I asked a tall Texan dressed in overalls.

"Sure am."

"But how do you know?"

"I'm the engineer."

I had picked the precise restaurant and had reached the precise room in the restaurant, just in time to hear just the conversation I needed to hear. I could have missed it if I had stopped in one of those other places or decided to take my chances on the Chinese food in the other room. It was as though I had been nudged to this spot. Maybe God speaks with a Texas drawl.

The big engineer came over to my table and spoke reassuringly. "It won't really leave at six-thirty. It won't be before nine in the morning. Anyway, they can't go without me."

He hesitated, then asked, "Where are you staying tonight?"

"Where are *you* staying?" I asked in return.

"Right here at the Sunday Inn. The whole crew's here." So I registered at the Sunday Inn as well. It seemed the smart thing to do. The congenial engineer stood beside me at the hotel desk. "My name is Pete Prater," he said.

"Glad to meet you, Pete," I said with gratitude. *I'm sticking with the engineer,* I thought. *If I miss this train I won't get out of town until the next train on Saturday night at 10:14.*

It wasn't until 9:10 the next morning that the Sunset Limited pulled in from El Paso, eleven hours late. The incoming conductor stepped off the train and said, "No passengers." I was the only passenger on the platform, standing there with Pete and the crew, so he must have been talking to me. I just looked at him, not knowing what to do. I knew it was four hundred miles looking east to San Antonio and more than three hundred fifty miles looking west to El Paso—with not much in between.

The new conductor, now about to step on board, said, "We're not going to leave this man standing here," as he waved me aboard. But then he told me, when I climbed up, "You've got two choices. You can wait for the next train going west to El Paso in a few hours, or you can stay on this train. But I've got to warn you, this train will have no air conditioning, no working bathrooms, no water. It's late because there's not enough power to service the train. You'll bake your way in a moving oven for four hundred miles across the desert."

I thought for a moment. *What do I do now?* Then I decided: "I'm going with you." A song from an old musical kept running through my mind, but with a Texas twist: "Once you have found a friend in the desert, *never* let him go." So I followed the conductor through the train. I was the only paying passenger aboard a twelve-car superliner, the prior passengers all having been removed at Tucson.

"You've got the train to yourself," said the conductor. "Pick the best roomette you can find, and it's all yours."

"What about the bathrooms?"

"I tell you what. None of them will flush. So you can just start at the rear of the train and use each one until you reach the front."

I picked the coolest bedroom I could find and then walked from car to car, from the deserted lounge to the sleepers and through the coaches, exploring my newfound empty home. It was like walking through a ghost train that was slipping noiselessly through a desert scene.

I returned to the dining car where the crew was hanging out, along with enough food for four hundred passengers. The food was slowly defrosting and we ate what we needed before it spoiled. We were slowly heating up, too, the sweat popping out on our faces. After a while I took off my shirt in my spacious sleeping car and changed to a pair of shorts.

"I hope you don't mind," I said when I returned to the dining car.

"Not in the least," said the conductor, by now a friend in mutual adversity.

We rolled on across the desert, the overheated silence broken by the computer voice on the conductor's radio. "SP detector 327," the computer said in a calm recorded female voice. "No defects," her automated voice added.

Oh? I thought.

I walked back through the empty train. It was silent except for the click of the rails. There was a rush of hot air when I squeezed my fingers into the rubber grommet around the doors to slide them open, one by one, all the way to the rear car. The door at the end of the last car was open, a red flag propped into the doorframe. The shimmering tracks were appearing from under the train, sliding out away from me with immeasurable speed and merging into one track at the horizon. *This is high adventure,* I thought. And then it occurred to me that Billie would have loved being here.

Maybe she was here.

But I hadn't really thought much of Billie since she died. Not the way I had thought about Dad and Jeff.

My goal had simply been the last bathroom on the train, and this had to be it—unless I counted the open doorway. An intriguing challenge. So I decided to try it out, and set a modern-day record. *Nobody has done that on the Sunset Limited!* I said to myself, with male satisfaction.

I returned to my writing desk in the lower bedroom of my sleeper, immersing myself in my written thoughts, trying to write between the small jerks of the train's motion. Then, almost imperceptibly, the motion slowed and came to a silent stop. I looked out the window. We were sitting on a railroad siding, waiting at a red light on the desert. It was so quiet you could hear the heat expanding the car's metal walls. I had sought a quiet place to write and I had certainly found it, sweating out the words one by one as I wrote in virtual isolation.

By the time we reached San Antonio after four hundred miles and eight hot hours, I was ready for a break.

The train crew had radioed ahead to take care of me. The agent met me at the station and shook my hand.

"I have the authority to make arrangements for you. What do you need?"

"If you'll get me a room for the night and a plane to Mobile tomorrow I'll appreciate it." So I ate spaghetti on San Antonio's famous River Walk, then spent the night recovering from near heat exhaustion. I noticed that the cool room didn't move an inch.

Episode V: Fairhope on Mobile Bay

When the plane wheels touched down at Mobile's modern airport I was in for a delightful little surprise at the car rental desk.

"I've got a red Probe waiting for you at the weekend rate," the agent said.

Ah, a Probe!

"It's a deal," I said, smiling.

My destination: Fairhope, an exceptional east-shore family town created by some hardworking Illinois farmers who were looking for a change in their lifestyle. They had picked a spot where you could watch the sun set virtually in the water.

The next morning, sitting at the end of a tin-roofed dock on the eastern shore of Mobile Bay at Fairhope, listening to the clattering rain on the tin, feeling the cooling breeze of the thunderstorm on a lazy Sunday afternoon, I looked back toward shore at an old wood-frame Catholic church I had attended an hour earlier. Inside, narrow white wainscoting covers the walls and ceilings. There is a porch on the bayside so people can come from communion in the church to communion with the water just a few feet away.

The clouds, the tin-tapping rain, and the slapping sound of the waves were speaking a message of peace, but I knew it hadn't always been this way here. The church steeple blew off in a tornado a few years back. The bell crashed to the ground, and the parishioners decided that neither the bell nor the steeple should go back on top. The bell now hung from a short wooden frame down near the ground, the bell rope hanging in easy reach for the people to ring as they come out of communion. As I wrote and watched at the end of the service, several children came out and rang the bell slowly. Then all the families walked back in the bright sun to their cars or bicycled their way home down the beach. It seemed a pleasant and secure way of life.

I was thankful that my friend Scott McTaggart, who lived in Fairhope, had found this extraordinary spot for me to write. He hadn't thought of the church until we were about to pass it.

"Here's a place," he said, swerving into the driveway. "We'll see if the Father is here."

The Reverend Charles Bordanca came out of a small rectory next door to the white church.

"Can my friend write here?" Scott asked.

"Sure. Right over there on the dock," he said, pointing out into the bay.

"May I come and take communion tomorrow?" I asked, aware that Protestants were technically barred from receiving the elements in Roman Catholic churches.

He looked at me. "How do you feel about that?" he asked.

"I feel good about it if you do."

"The important thing is relationship," he said. "Relationship happens when we let God do God's work and we do people's work. We don't need to try to do God's work, and we don't need to pretend anything or try to be good by ourselves. Jesus took care of all that for us. We just need to live in Him."

"Good," my friend Scott said. "If you go to the eight o'clock mass, I will be serving you."

Scott a Vietnam vet who studied for the priesthood but then was called to business. Now he was pleased at the opportunity to administer the sacraments of the church to me, and I was pleased to receive them. So today at the early mass I stood before my friend and listened to him say to me in a hushed tone, "The body of Jesus Christ." I received it just as the priest instructed and said, "Amen." It was the same sense of awe I had experienced at the words of the priest in Rome when he said, "Corpus Christi."

Now, hours later, writing alone on this dock in a retreating thunderstorm, I sensed the healing of the Lord in this peaceful place. This time it was healing I hadn't known I needed, and it had to do with Billie.

I remembered how she had often explained her love of her quiet place overlooking Long Lake. "I go out on the porch swing at the end of the day and watch the sun light up a path of diamonds across the water to the shore."

Suddenly I realized I had not taken the time to really miss Billie. I had been so caught up in the remarkable timing of her leaving, and agreeing with it, that I had not shed one tear. Now, to my surprise, forty feet from shore on a Fairhope dock, I broke down, my weeping echoing the splashing of the last raindrops into the bay.

"I miss you, Billie," I was saying. "Billie, I miss you. . . . Billie. . . ."

She had always responded to water and now I was doing the same, with the heritage of an old white church in view and the sound of the old bell still ringing in my memory. After all the other quiet places I had sought and enjoyed, I began to understand better what quietness can do. I guess I remembered the old white church and the bell I had heard so often in my childhood. Most of us have a vision or a bell from our childhood. And it rings softly in our hearts once in a while.

We must come to a quiet place to really remember our loved ones. And we need a quiet place to let them go. In the silent moment after the storms of life, the Lord speaks. And when we finally listen, the healing comes. So much goes on in quiet places.

Next day I caught the early train that moves graciously up from the water level of Mobile Bay to Birmingham and on to Atlanta, Charlotte, Washington, and New York. It was somewhere in Alabama that I began to realize what I had been suffering from—what I had gradually been finding healing for—in the new views from my window and the new friends along the way, and the silent times for writing and thinking.

I'd heard about depression but wouldn't have wanted to admit to it years ago if it had happened to me. Now I could see the symptoms were real: inability to break out of lethargy, unexplained fatigue, a feeling of being stalled in my tracks, unable to complete the big things I had scheduled, only the little meaningless things that the daily schedule demands. The inability to see God in much of anything or hear anything but the empty silence within.

Depression can creep into a person's life so quietly and just take over. Nothing seems to be wrong physically. You eat, sleep, work, and slowly wind down into vague dissatisfaction. You say, "Everything's just fine." But your life has jumped the track. And you get back on the right track only when you recognize everything isn't all right—even when you don't know why.

There is more than one way to confront depression. Many people go to a counselor. Some may need medication to correct some sort of physical chemical imbalance. In my case, I believe the imbalance was at least partly spiritual—an ego problem brought on by self-preoccupation. It was a matter of feeling sorry for myself but not admitting it—even to myself. I was only listening to me. But my therapy of choice, a train trip, had worked because it gave me something outside myself to focus on, to listen to—and in the process, gave me the space to focus on my deepest self. All the way around America I had been making my slow, tunneling escape from the prison of silent self-sorrow.

"See God in everything," the beautiful black man had said. Now I was finally able to see again—and I was being healed.

Aha! Sunrise—in my soul.

Rumbling on through America, I passed through the middle South, then the cities of the Northeast. Finally my train approached Manhattan's tall jumble of buildings. Now I was approaching New York from a new perspective, coming from the West, not from the east side where I had seen the message in the moving train window years ago. This time the train stood a remarkably short time in the dark underground station before moving on and out to the east side of the city. It emerged from the tunnel under the river into Queens, slowly arching its way around and drawing parallel to the parade of buildings out my left window.

I looked for Jeff's hospital but strangely couldn't spot it. My new vision was now focused on my final destination, Stamford, Connecticut, where Joan was waiting for me. And an hour later there she was, standing on the platform when my train rolled in. She was as exciting to see as she was in the Schenectady train station nearly forty years ago. She was dressed in pink, smiling silently as she walked toward me. I dropped the handle of my suitcase and reached out to her with both arms.

"Welcome home," she whispered in my ear. And then we said nothing. We didn't need to. We knew.

You can hear the silent language of people you love and see the presence of God in them. It is right in front of you. All around you. Within you.

And if for some reason your eyes and ears become blocked by pain or loss or depression then you need to do something. Do whatever it takes, even if it's difficult or expensive or inconvenient. (It wasn't easy to shut down my business for my extended train ride.) Ask for help if you need it. Beg for help if necessary. But life is too short, relationships too precious, God's messages too vital to risk not hearing them.

But my healing was not over when I got home to Connecticut and Pound Ridge after that long train journey. Even then I had another healing coming, the healing of the underlying *cause* of my depression and my confusion in life.

After all, I had come to live the words of the beautiful maintenance man, "See God in everything." And I had seen God in the death of Dad and Jeff and Billie. But now I needed to see—*through* my windows into the wisdom and purpose of God in my own life. I needed to see God better and I had to get out of the past to do it.

8

GIVERS AND FORGIVERS

VOICES AMONG THE TOMBSTONES

"But the wisdom from above is first pure, then peaceable, gentle, open to reason, full of mercy."

—The Book of James

I met Tom Facelle at a committee meeting. We didn't know it, but we had more in common than committee membership. Both of us had lost a son to death.

We met again at a men's weekend held at a rugged camp in New York's Catskill Mountains, and this is where we forged a friendship, on a spiritual retreat. On Saturday night I was to give a brief account of what I had learned through the death of my son, and Tom encouraged me as I voiced my fears over saying the wrong thing.

"Think of it this way," Tom said as we walked from the lodge. "God is the ventriloquist and you are the dummy. Let God do the talking."

That was a help to me. I had been writing about listening to the silent language of God and seeing God in everything throughout my train trip around America, and here was a friend saying in effect, "You don't even need to hear the voice. Just open your mouth, and things will be said through you."

His words were expanding the message "See God in everything" into a new idea: "Let others see God through you."

So I rested on that advice, knowing that I had another day before my turn came to speak.

That evening Tom and I went to an overflowing auditorium that the camp calls the Town Hall. We sat on the floor in a crowded section of the stage, but the young man next to me offered me his chair. He must have looked at my silver hair and decided I needed special treatment.

"No thanks. I'm fine," I said. But when we stood to participate in a rousing song, our voices booming through the room, the young man slipped his chair behind me. "There," he said as I discovered it in sitting down, "I gotcha."

He was a clean-cut young man whose sensitivity showed beautifully when we were given an opportunity to share some feelings in a group of three. Tom and I listened to the young man voice his extraordinary desire to be a husband who was not just interested in making money. He stood with quiet tears on his face as he voiced his deep concern and I was struck with the strength of his vulnerability. He was about the age my son had been when he died.

"What's your name?" I asked.

"Jeff," I thought he said. *Jeff! Could that be? Was I imagining? Or did he just seem to be Jeff?* In so many ways he was like him, in another body.

I had begun to learn that such apparent coincidences of daily life are often not coincidences at all. So Tom and I listened to him. I listened with a special ear.

The following night I was called to the lectern to speak to two hundred and fifty men packed from wall to wall. I had a general idea of what I was supposed to say, but I had struggled with how vulnerable I should be. Men don't like to cry, certainly not in front of several hundred of their peers. But I remembered that I was to be the dummy and allow God to be the ventriloquist. I knew I would hear what I was to say only when I said it. So I started speaking, believing that the words would be what they were supposed to be.

"When my father died of cancer in September of that year," I said, "I could handle it, because that's the way it's supposed to be. Fathers are supposed to die before their sons. But I missed my father that night at midnight when I went out on the dock in the little Adirondack town of Long Lake. I called out to the cold black sky, 'Dad.' But there was no answer. I cried a little, then, standing at the edge of the dock, looking down at the black water. But I could handle it because I saw the little pinpricks of light we see as stars, as though they were part of one great comforting light peeking through the pinholes in some giant black umbrella."

I paused.

"It was when my son died the next month of the same cancer that I couldn't handle it."

I broke off, unable to continue. The auditorium fell silent. Strong emotions were rippling across the faces of the men, now riveted to their places on the floor, across the stage, and in the entryway. I don't remember all the things I said then, because they were not my words.

Ten minutes later I concluded, saying, "The older I get, the more I appreciate the things in life that sound simple. Simple words like 'Jesus loves me. This I know.' "

The roomful of men was motionless, but filled wall to wall with unspoken power. As I threaded my way back to my seat, a man reached out his hand and gripped mine. Another reached up and asked if he could talk with me later. My friend Tom stood and hugged me with tears in his eyes, remembering his own son who had committed suicide, and two hundred and fifty men stood up with him.

It is the willingness to be vulnerable that makes men learn from each other—to respond to a stranger, to learn how to become friends, to see God in someone else's circumstance.

A young man so like Jeff had started it the night before, and now the contagion of vulnerability set the stage for Tom Facelle and me to make a pact. That weekend, together we would make a pilgrimage to visit our sons' graves, only a few miles apart. In the process, we hoped, we would share each other's wisdom and somehow grow into a deeper understanding of our lives and our losses.

It was a blustery autumn day when Tom and I set out on our shared journey, carrying with us our lifetimes of experience. Together, we embodied the fields of law and justice, military expertise, business management, corporate training, writing, and the life roles of father, son, and spouse.

Tom, a retired Supreme Court Justice for the state of New York, a retired Air Force General, and a devout Catholic, had enlisted in the army at age seventeen. His mother died a year later. Tom worked his way through college and law school when his service hitch was through. His early life had not been easy, but later he had experienced a rewarding and varied career.

I had grown up in an economically deprived but spiritually rewarding home, a country parsonage, before joining the Air Force and then IBM. I started at the bottom in the company and then worked my way up through several divisions, in the process traveling worldwide and writing several books. After thirty years I retired from IBM's Corporate Management Development Center. There I had created, taught, and managed development programs for IBM trainers and managers around the world. As with Tom, my life had become increasingly easy. I had received an honorary doctorate, and my management consulting business had blossomed with little effort. Now Tom and I were bringing both of these fruitful, satisfying lives to the graves of our sons, both knowing that our losses had changed us deeply, wondering now what meaning we might find in sharing our losses.

We approached expansive Gate of Heaven Cemetery through an impressive portal and saw hundreds of markers dotting the many low hills below us. We descended to the Facelle family plot and stood looking at the stone. That's when I learned that our sons had been close in age. Tom's son, Bob, had died at age thirty. Jeff had been twenty-nine. And they had died just months apart.

I read the words inscribed on the stone. "Safely home in God's care."

Tom looked at me. "Don, the words on the stone have a special meaning for me because my son took his own life after a long and stormy bout with drugs. There was nothing we could do to save him. We tried everything, including something called Tough Love. In the end Bob came home in the only way he knew, by ending his life."

We were silent for a while before Tom continued.

"For me, the death of my son was God's way of releasing him from a tormented life that I couldn't do anything about and never will understand."

Tom looked at me again. "You have fond memories of your dad and your son and your mother, and you drew closer to each of them as they were dying. I didn't have that chance. My mother died before I got home from the army. And my son ended his life in our home while I was in the hospital for surgery."

I looked at Tom as he finished. I could only imagine the desolation he must have felt then. But there was no heaviness in Tom's spirit as he continued softly.

"Now I have come to a place of peace, Don. I know that God only loaned me my son and He has called him back to his heavenly home. That's why the inscription on this gravestone says 'Safely home.'"

We stood talking a long while in the wind of the autumn day, the fallen leaves swirling around the stones. Wisdom comes from painful experience, not from ease. And I was privileged to hear the wisdom that Tom's pain had earned him.

Now, driving to Jeff's cemetery, I continued to listen. The inscription on Bob's gravestone came from a poem that contained other words of deep meaning to Tom. "Try to look beyond earth's shadows," he quoted to me. And "There is work still waiting for you."

There had been other moments of preparation in Tom's life. When he was receiving one of the last briefings at the Pentagon, upon his promotion to Brigadier General, Tom heard a four-star general say, "Gentlemen, there will come a time after all your honors when you will stand in another meeting. You will be stripped of all your medals. You will stand naked at the end of your life looking at God. And how will you answer Him when He asks, 'What have you done for me?'"

Tom finished his story. "No one clapped, Don," he said. "We all filed out of the room, unable to respond."

Such rare visions and such voices of wisdom, now silent in the passing of time, still linger in our ears and stand in our minds for years. They are strong gifts of words that never go away. And in still moments with friends and strangers, and loved ones, we have the privilege of drawing such gifts out of our past and passing them on.

Now we were getting closer to Jeff's resting place in quiet Connecticut. As we drove, Tom reflected on his life as a judge.

"I am no longer impressed by a judge's flowing robes as he steps into the courtroom. It doesn't mean much now to have heard my name announced as the Honorable Judge Thomas Facelle. The sweep of the robes and the bang of the gavel can be just an ego trip."

After a moment Tom took out his wallet and read a morning prayer by an unknown author that meant more to him—and to me—than titles, occupations, or the author's name.

Morning Prayer

O God, this new day opens before us
with promise and opportunity.
It is your gift to us;
help us to make it our gift to you.
The day lies before us
like a page waiting to be written.
Save us from scribbling over it
meaningless marks and idle doodling.
Help us to write somewhere upon it
a poem of praise,
a prayer of compassion,
a significant sentence—
Help us to say less and to mean more,
to make gestures of grace and not of haste.
Give us good words to speak,
good thoughts to think,
good deeds to do.
But above all, evoke from us praise,
that we may be the best of all givers:
thanksgivers.
In Jesus' name. Amen

118

As we approached the country place where Jeff was buried, the little cemetery rose above a quiet road beyond a narrow bridge. A split-rail fence enclosed the few gravestones. The sky was overcast, and a hint of autumn chilled the air as we walked to Jeff's grave on the windy hillside. Now we stood together by the stone as Tom read the inscription,

"With Jesus, even the darkness is full of light."

After a long silence we looked out on a barn in the field below and remarked how good it would be if the sun came out.

Instantly, it did.

For one moment the sun shone squarely in our faces as we stood facing the silent message chiseled in stone. For one brief moment the cold stone and the cool day were punctuated by the warmth of the sun. Then the sun slipped back behind the cloud cover. We looked again at the words etched in the gravestone: "Even the darkness is full of light."

"You saw that?" I asked.

"Yes."

"We were just standing here, speaking of the light, and it came."

"I know."

What do you say when even the movement of nature seems to speak? It fit with what the maintenance man had said: "See God in everything."

Tom stepped to the stone and placed his hand on it without saying anything.

"Do you want to say some words, Tom, before we go?"

"I just did," he said quietly, looking at me.

We left, comforted, aware of the light. I remembered that a similar light had also suddenly shined through the church window at Jeff's funeral five years earlier. Then the light had moved slowly along the floor as the funeral continued. At the end of the funeral, it lit up the top of the casket. In both instances the timing of the light had been precise.

How many messages we miss by labeling them as coincidence! I believe we are meant to recognize the quiet communications of our Lord. We are to put the unspoken pieces together, those from the timing of the clouds, from the deep unspoken prayers of our friends, from the still stones in front of us that speak out in silent power. "With Jesus, even the darkness is full of light."

And from the indelible words of a stranger, softly spoken, yet lasting a lifetime: "See God in everything."

As we drove from the cemetery Tom commented on our cycle of life, on the birth, growth, and death of our children and of ourselves while life goes on from generation to generation. "This cycle is to be received with thanksgiving, Don," he said. And together we gave thanks as we headed toward home.

After all my travels to other countries and around America, this was the real turning point toward the future. Our voices among the gravestones, on the way to and from the cemeteries of our sons, the messages of the chiseled words in stone, the timing of the sunlight, the litany in my mind of the maintenance man's words—all these voices now were coming home, turning me from self-preoccupation to facing a question spoken in God's silent language: "I have done all this for you. What have you done for me?"

God's messages unfold in so many layers. We think we understand the real messages of life, only to find later that we were just being prepared for the real level of understanding beneath. It's like stepping on an elevator at the top floor of a grand hotel, pushing the button for the ground floor, and stopping at the mezzanine, thinking you've reached the street. The real ground floor is one floor down and the foundation is even farther below. When we recognize where our real ground is we must occupy it. Patiently, one floor at a time.

Home from my cemetery pilgrimage, I came across one of Jeff's letters to himself, written while he was dying in the hospital. It said:

> More and more now, I think of what my life has amounted to recently, and I see a mixture of good things and bad. . . . I wanted to build up more money, more things. . . . I wanted to live my life in its free and easy, unencumbered mode. This free and easy mode, however, has been a license to put my work above its proper place and has also been a

sort of self-centered trap . . . but the question is what is God's intended best for us?

Fresh from the experience of looking back over my life, I was deeply struck by Jeff's words. A self-centered trap, or self-preoccupation, versus God's intended best for us, makes us a double prisoner—a jailbird wearing a blindfold and earplugs. When we take off the blindfold and unblock our ears, then we can find our way out of prison. Self-preoccupation, whether through tragedy, or success, actually keeps us from seeing our true calling in a troubled age marked by self-concern. Instead of putting on a new life of vision, power, and thanksgiving, we imprison ourselves in loss.

Then I stumbled across several extraordinary letters to Jeff from Cambodian children whom Jeff and his wife, Lindy, had taught, and their signatures are as foreign to my ears as their letters are beautiful: Pekom and Vanna, Kin Phay, Samileang, Bunsong, Chhin Chhay, and Savong. I remember Savong. She was a beautiful little girl with a winsome smile. Her letter to Jeff said, "We all misses you very much and some of the kids worries too. I worries the most."

Another letter—a note, when writing became the way Jeff communicated with Lindy as he was losing the battle:

> I love you!
> I'm sorry I was quite cranky!
> So demanding . . .
> Sometimes.
> But you have been terrific at night.
> Taking a little longer to recover.
> I think Tony put his needle in deeper than last there.
> I feel it more.
> Can you read slower?
> Can you
> Put your warm hands on my back?
> No need to move them—
> It's very soothing for my lungs.
> Did I ask too much today?
> Hands a little lower,
> Left hand over left lung,
> Yes!

Five years later I can read these intimate thoughts and understand the larger message of my son who wrote about putting work above its intended place. But even in his last, painful days he was working his way out of self and into a new perspective. And teaching me now, five years later.

So many of us spend our lives discovering our identity in our work, then deriving our identity from our work and finally deluding ourselves into thinking that our worth is in our work. But the moving Presence of our Lord constantly speaks, in His language, not in ours. And the message is always the same.

Jeff heard the message, and he responded to it:

We find our real worth in relationship, not in achievement.

We don't need to prove ourselves to God in order to be loved. He isn't impressed with titles like Judge, General, Author, Doctor, President. He isn't impressed by *anything* we achieve. He is crazy about *us*. He likes it when we are honest, vulnerable, real in our feelings—without judging others or even ourselves. He likes it when we come from a low place, not a haughty place. That is when the deepest insight and creativity comes. When we are at the peak of our performance, directing our private world, or when we are laid low—at all times He works for a one-to-one relationship that is unique to Him and to us as individuals.

This is the meaning in Jeff's life and death. This is the message he heard and responded to, the message I must hear in his absence and ongoing presence. I am to see beyond my family to others.

I must go beyond looking and listening for God's silent language. I must learn to listen to the needs of others.

9

ONE CROOKED FINGER

HOW LESLIE CAME HOME

"Blessed are the pure in heart, for they shall see God."

—The Gospel of Matthew

Leslie was single, alone, and searching for something. Her real name isn't Leslie, but that's what we began to call her on Christmas Day when she first visited Joan and me.

We were looking for a good movie on television, and I scanned *The New York Times* television guide in the semidarkness of early evening. "Here's one," I said, trying to make out the title in the subdued lighting of our family room. "It's called *Leslie, Come Home.*"

"Are you sure it's not *Lassie, Come Home?*" Joan asked. And Leslie broke out in uncontrollable laughter.

That was the beginning of a friendship that soon grew beyond laughter. It had to grow beyond that. Within a few weeks Leslie had admitted herself to a psychiatric hospital, a brave thing to do when she didn't know what was causing her to think of suicide. There was no apparent reason for these dark thoughts. She was bright, young, successful, an intensive-care nurse in a highly esteemed hospital. She had a promising future. But something was going wrong, and she knew it.

In the hospital she began to get an inkling of what the problem was. In group therapy she began to remember what she did not want to believe. It was a memory so painful that she had blocked it out of her conscious mind many years before. *No, it couldn't have happened. How could it happen? Not him—he couldn't do that to me. It must not be true. It isn't true. . . .*

It was too terrifying even to want to remember. So Leslie had buried her harsh memories deep within, covering them up with unfathomable despair. Now, when she finally remembered, bitter anger engulfed her.

"Where were you, God?" she asked in bitter anger. "Where were you when a five-year-old girl needed you?"

But recognition, group therapy, rage at God, screaming in the silent room—these did little more than drive Leslie closer to despair. The scratches on her wrists showed increasing fury, frightening her further. Finally there was little choice but to transfer to another hospital.

In the maximum-security ward, everything was taken away to save Leslie's life. The imprisonment of precautions reduced her days to fighting the nurses, rejecting food, hiding in the covers of her bed, fighting life itself. Dull daily grayness had replaced the bright laughter of our first Leslie experience.

We visited Leslie often, caught up now in her struggle, buoyed by her occasional smiles, encouraged by glimpses of an underlying love of laughter. We believed it was that laughter that could somehow forge a link with another life. But laughter was drowned daily with fury.

"I don't want to see my parents. Not now, not ever," she commanded her hospital helpers in the one remaining area she could command, cutting off ties with her natural family.

Our phone rang one morning. "Hello, Pops."

Hearing Leslie's greeting I knew I was more than a good friend. I had raised four sons her age or older. Now, for a while at least, I had a daughter named Leslie. A bright, brave, colorful daughter who was in the process of withering away from pain and fury.

The only thing Leslie seemed to respond to was laughter, and an occasional hug from a selected few. How do you reach a person who has been hurt to the point of desperate isolation? How do you relate to her grief when your own experience has been entirely different? Do you just stand beside her?

Maybe, I thought. *Maybe there is a way.* It was a slow-forming idea.

After I gave a talk about seeing God in everything, my friend Howard decided to give me a gift. He cast those words of advice in beautiful calligraphy and carefully framed them with a light blue mat. The words stood out fresh and strong again for me in that striking setting. I placed them on my desk, facing the door, so the message greeted me in the morning, advised me in the evening, stood waiting for me during the day.

Could these words come to mean something to both Leslie and me? Would Leslie feel that the words were a superficial wish, brought just to be nice—or a cruel mockery to someone paralyzed with silent loneliness? Would my intended help sink Leslie deeper into depression?

I had come to realize years before that there is no relationship without risk. So I brought the framed words with me to Leslie's hospital. I pushed the button beside the heavy glass inner door of the acute-care unit and watched the staff person through the thick glass as she reached for the intercom button.

"Yes?"

"Osgood. To see Leslie." But I used Leslie's real name, because the nursing staff would not have understood our private nickname.

"All right."

The high-pitched whistle signaled that the door was unlocked, holding its pitch until I entered. It stopped automatically as I entered, relocking the door. Then I held up the framed words to the staff person, knowing what her response might be.

"This glass cannot be brought in," she directed. Then in a moment, looking at the words, "But the picture can."

I removed the glass and left it with the nurse. Leslie's room was subdued in the early evening darkness. She was buried under the covers.

"Leslie?"

"Yes?"

"I've brought you something."

There was no movement.

"It's a loan, Leslie. Something special a friend of mine made. A little sign with some special words that mean a lot to me."

She was not interested.

"When you are ready, I'll show it to you."

No interest.

Switching my approach, I offered an alternative, trying to intrigue her. "Before I leave I'll show it to you." Silence.

"You can't have it," I said, watching carefully for a reaction. "You can only borrow it."

Then, surprisingly, we began to talk, for nearly two hours. Our conversation was punctuated by anger, silence, and surprising bursts of real laughter whenever we remembered the gift of good humor.

Then, out of a brief silence she spoke softly, surprising me.

"I . . . don't want to die."

Her words had quietly entered the room. They rose delicately to my ears from the bed covers. Five fragile words were a pinpoint of light developing in a darkroom. But there was not much more. Healing comes slowly, in the smallest change, the softest word, much like the quiet words spoken to me in a hospital five years before. "See God in everything." And now I was trying to say them too.

But that was all for now, except an honest hug for Joan. Leslie really felt closer to Joan than she did to me, but still she hugged me at the door.

That quiet flicker of hope didn't develop into healing for Leslie, at least not yet. Shortly afterward, Leslie's condition took a turn downward, and no one could stop her plunge into darkness again. Then her benefits ran out, and she could no longer afford to stay in the private hospital. They extended her another week while her counselor, Joan, and I, and other concerned people explored other possibilities. Finally the hospital authorities said she might have to be committed to a state mental institution.

News of this shattered Leslie, who alternated between rational thought and near immobility. The idea of Leslie in the state institution jarred all of us; it seemed like a life sentence to prison. But the days were running out, and we had no other answer.

But there was one slim chance. If Leslie could prove to them that she was not suicidal, if she could prove it to them for one week, they would let her go to a friend's house, where there might be enough care and love to help her pull through.

In those few days many people prayed for Leslie, for someone they hardly knew. And four nights later our phone rang.

"Hello, Pops. Are you sitting down?"

"Yes, Leslie. I'm sitting down."

"Listen to me. They're going to let me come home!"

Leslie was speaking as though she had just climbed to the top of some mountain and she was making a statement to the buffeting winds of life, "I can go home!"

"That's great news, Leslie. And we're ready for you to come . . . home."

There never was a question between Joan and me that "home" for Leslie would be with us. It just seemed right, though we were concerned about the fact that we didn't have the professional expertise to help her.

"Just give her the loving family that she lacks," the hospital authorities told us.

"You know our home is not suicide-proof."

"Yes. But she has convinced us that it will not occur."

We thought of all the questions you could think, yet none of the possible answers deterred us. Sometimes you just know what you have to do, even when you don't quite understand it.

So, on the day Leslie was to be released, I drove over to Connecticut. It was a bright spring morning as the sun bathed the lush Connecticut neighborhoods and the discreetly hidden grounds of the institution. Now standing in front of the heavy glass, I rang the bell, anticipating the moment.

"Yes?"

"Osgood. To pick up Leslie." But I used her real name again.

They buzzed me in, and Leslie was waiting in the lobby, radiating expectation. Her room had already been reassigned to someone else.

"I'm ready," she said. "I've been ready."

Stepping through the heavy door to the fresh green of the bright spring day, Leslie drank in the cool morning air. I remembered how Jeff looked when we were able to take him out of the hospital for a few hours. It was an afternoon like this. When his bare feet touched the ground he breathed a word of quiet joy at the mere touch of grass. Then I appreciated, as I never had, the fresh gift of touch, the bright gift of color, the sweetness of the air. We forget the gifts we are given until we are in prospect of losing them.

Now, as we drove through the clean Connecticut countryside, Leslie kept up a steady thanksgiving for the sun-filled ride. She looked at the passing scene through her open window, breathing in the faint scent of new leaves and spring grass.

It is a gift to see someone appreciate the simplicity of freedom. It was a gift to see Leslie come home.

But it was not easy for Leslie to learn to live free again, to return to good health. There were still many days of heaviness, confusion, and the recurring despair that had to be faced again and again in her resolve to be healed.

Leslie's therapist cautioned me not to press for healing too quickly, not to give advice or to say things like, "You can be healed if you learn to forgive." There is an optimum time and the right place to suggest such things, and this wasn't the time. Besides, it really wasn't my job. Leslie's therapist was looking for deeper healing, the kind that comes from really digging down inside, exposing the anger and the full cause of it, so that the depression wouldn't recur later in life.

Meanwhile, my role, and Joan's, was to be a helping presence rather than a counselor. It was time for me to practice patience. But it wasn't easy. I like to take action, to solve problems, to see progress. And sometimes I wondered if Leslie was making any progress at all.

As the days went on I made several signs in different typestyles, from Mixage to Old English Text to Symbol. Though some of the signs were hard to read, all the signs said the same thing.

SEE GOD IN EVERYTHING
SEE GOD IN EVERYTHING
SEE GOD IN EVERYTHING
SEE GOD IN EVERYTHING
SEE GOD IN EVERYTHING
ΣΕΕ ΓΟΔ ΙΝ ΕςΕΡΨΤΗΙΝΓ

But while I had found profound meaning and comfort in learning to see God and listen in to His silent language, Leslie had trouble with this concept. She didn't hear anything at all from God, and she wasn't sure she wanted to. And she could find no comfort in thinking of God as her loving heavenly Father. Fathers were not a welcome subject for Leslie to think about or talk about at all.

Sometimes Leslie seemed to be pulling up slowly from the deep canyons of her depression, but her progress wasn't steady. She would climb higher, little by little, then slip back down again. It was hard to tell, but we thought she was moving up. The special prayers at the church on Saturdays, the visits to the counselors, the jokes and the moments of laughter, our commitment to be a loving family, Leslie's ongoing bravery in facing her nightmares— all these were mingled together in our daily lives. There was no sequence other than the sequence of life.

But the months stretched into seasons, the seasons stretched into a year . . . and on into the second year before something decisive happened. It was that long before real change occurred, and even then it did not happen as we supposed. It came as a clap of thunder rather than the bright sunrise we had hoped for. But God speaks in the thunder as much as He does in the sunshine.

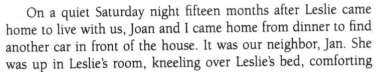

On a quiet Saturday night fifteen months after Leslie came home to live with us, Joan and I came home from dinner to find another car in front of the house. It was our neighbor, Jan. She was up in Leslie's room, kneeling over Leslie's bed, comforting her, watching over her.

"She took too many of these," Jan told us in her gentle way, handing me a bottle of pills. "I counted what was left."

The label on the bottle said, "One, at bedtime."

"How many did she take?"

"I'm not sure, but I think seven. She says they're not life-threatening, but when she called me she was so frightened that I rushed right over."

I hurried downstairs and called the poison control center.

It was a man's voice. "Seven? She took seven pills? Is she trying to hurt herself? That's a lot of pills!"

"There is a history behind this," I said, taking care not to mention Leslie's name.

"My official advice to you is to get her to the emergency room right away."

"She's a nurse, and she says the pills are not life-threatening."

His voice repeated the same message. "My official advice is to take her to the emergency room. But if she won't go to the hospital, give her something to eat to absorb the rest of the drug's effect."

We got Leslie downstairs and fed her something, but she couldn't keep it down.

"Well, that got rid of the poison!" Jan said. "I think she'll be all right now."

I brought the rest of the pills into our room. Joan and I went to bed that night, confident that Leslie was out of danger, but shaken that she was still so fragile after all this time.

All Joan and I could do was shake our heads, pray, attempt to discern God's leading. We honestly didn't know what to do.

Leslie seemed better the next day, and she was already in bed that night when Joan and I came in from an evening engagement. We felt good that she was resting. But the phone rang for Leslie an hour or so after we came in. I knocked on her door. "It's a call from your cousin, Carol."

In about ten minutes the phone rang again, and I took the call on the portable phone downstairs. It was Carol, crying. "She's killing herself!"

"What?"

"She's in her room. She's taken thirty pills!"

"Hold on, Carol!" I rushed up the stairs with Joan right behind me. We pushed the door open and rushed to Leslie's bed, the portable phone still in my hand. "Leslie, Carol says you've taken pills! How many?"

She looked drowsy. "How many pills, Leslie?"

"Thirty," she drawled.

"Carol? Leslie's still awake. We're taking her to the emergency room . . . Soundview Hospital . . . Connecticut . . . right now! You can call there."

I put the phone down. "Into your robe, Leslie. No questions. No options. I'm calling the doctor to meet us at the emergency room."

The three of us careened down North Street, breaking the speed limits, passing slow-moving cars on a double center line. My mind was speeding ahead.

If a policeman stops us, I thought, *I'll just ask him to escort us.*

And I was also thinking, *This has to stop sometime.* All of my doubts and my impatience seemed to coalesce, my frustration coming to a head. I was tired of waiting for improvement. Maybe this was the time to turn Leslie over to more capable hands.

In the mystery of God's grace, I was both wrong and miraculously right.

———— ✑ ————

The hospital finally loomed above us. We left the car at the curb and raced into the emergency room. They were expecting us.

In bed quickly, Leslie was teary-eyed as I looked at her. She was already being fed a soupy charcoal mixture.

"We're leaving you here, Leslie," I said. "You'll be all right. They know what to do here. Your life is important, and that's what matters right now. But all past agreements are off. I'm calling your parents so they know where you are."

Leslie listened quietly and looked at me, waiting for me to say more.

"No one can help you more than you can help yourself, Leslie. Apparently, we're not helping you, so we're going to leave you to reflect on all this. You must take charge of your healing. There's not a person on this planet that can help you get better . . . until you decide you want to get better."

Leslie broke down. "You're just going to walk out . . . and leave me here?"

"Yes. The hospital people say you're going to be all right. But you don't seem to understand what you've done. This is serious. So serious that we've got to go away and think about whether we're good for you. Unwittingly, we may have become part of the problem."

"When will we talk? When will you come back?"

"We don't know, Leslie." Joan was calm, reassuring, but non-committal as she responded. "We've got to think about what's best for you. We're just going to leave you in better hands."

We walked out to the car, slid into the bucket seats and drove slowly back to Pound Ridge, talking in circles, trying to discern what we should do.

"We've got to leave her to God, Joan. She's got to come to the place where she knows who can help her, and it isn't us. We can't help her anymore. Only she can help, if she listens to the voice of God."

"Maybe so, Don." Joan's voice had a resignation in it. "I just need time to think through it all. . . ."

I had to leave for the Boar's Head Inn in Charlottesville, Virginia, for a two-day conference. Actually it was a reunion of the graduates of a leadership program called New Perspectives I had started for the DuPont Corporation. The timing for a reunion was good. I desperately needed a new perspective myself.

I had already received calls from the hospital psychiatrist and from Leslie's therapist. One voice on my recording machine said, "Mr. Osgood, we'll need to know what your plans are. It will affect what we do. We may be able to get a short period covered in a psychiatric institution, but it won't be long. Will you let her come back to your home? Otherwise she may be caught with no place to go."

I responded in the same way to both calls. "I don't know what

I will do. Part of Leslie's healing may be in the uncertainty of what will happen. I won't decide anything for a few days."

I felt strongly that Joan and I were to do nothing until we knew for sure. But deep inside, I was already feeling sure. I had convinced myself that we had to stand firm, that living with us was not in Leslie's best interest.

During the New Perspectives reunion—we call it "renewal"— we always reserve one evening for sharing whatever difficulties we are having as individuals. It's a time when anyone can say anything. It's a time for respect, for listening. I led the group with my perplexity over Leslie, telling my colleagues, "It seems the time has come for me to practice Tough Love. I believe it's time for me to require a young woman who has been living with us while recovering to live somewhere else where she can get the help she needs."

On the final morning of the renewal meeting at the Boar's Head Inn, I walked into the conference room, and people started coming up to me before the beginning of the meeting. They wanted to give me their thoughts about Leslie after the sharing meeting the night before.

"Are you sure of what you're doing?" one said.

"You've got to finish what you've started, what you're supposed to do," another told me.

One handed me his card with a note scrawled on the back: "Don, what would Jesus do?"

And then, once again, my perspective began to shift. Then I began to wonder how much of my Tough Love was motivated by concern for Leslie's best interest and how much by my impatience with uncertainty. I knew I cared about Leslie. But was I also reacting out of fear of being hurt, of once again losing a person I loved?

By noon, when I finished the program, I knew I had to do something about what my New Perspectives friends had said. I announced to the group, "I want you to know that I've listened to your individual concerns over Leslie and . . . I . . . want you to know that I'm going to pray for direction before deciding that Leslie can't come home."

Several of them gathered around me, giving expression to

their concern. It was a chorus of support, a remarkable message to reconsider my decision. Sometimes God whispers in someone else's ear, and they speak the words of God to us when we haven't been listening.

I went to my room and called my wife. "Leslie's important, Joan, and so are you. If you think we should let her come home, I'll agree. We'll talk with her again in thirty days and re-evaluate what we should do then."

But what happened to Leslie during this time? I won't be able to convey her innermost feelings, but I want to tell her story as Leslie told it to me. I have changed some of the names of people, places, and institutions so that I can protect the privacy of Leslie's family and friends.

Over the next few days after we left Leslie in the emergency room, while Joan and I were trying to decide what to do about bringing her home, Leslie was lying in a hospital room wondering what she had done to her life. Because of her attempted suicide she was never left alone. But she felt more alone than ever in her life.

A former nursing colleague was assigned to sit with Leslie all night. They talked on into the early hours of Sunday morning. Then another nurse friend named Lois came over for a while. For several months Lois had been encouraging Leslie to consider God, so it wasn't surprising that Lois said a prayer over Leslie when she came. It was just the natural thing for Lois to do.

Monday was Labor Day. The hospital psychiatrist came in to talk with Leslie about institutions that might be good for her. He mentioned Hillcrest, the private institution where Leslie had been before, but nothing could be done right away because the administrative people were away for the holiday weekend. Looking back, we can now see that this too was all part of an unseen, unspoken plan. I might call it a theatrical drama being played out, except it was real.

Another sitter came to sit with Leslie from seven on Monday morning until three that afternoon. She was a black woman who was pregnant. She was very cheerful. Her conversation was sprinkled with comments like "Praise the Lord" and "God is so good." That language just seemed to be a part of her. Leslie didn't think a lot about it. But when Leslie needed someone to talk with, she called a minister.

Neely Towe is the senior pastor at the church where Joan is the associate pastor. Leslie told Neely, "I'm afraid that what I've done has destroyed the only family relationship I ever really had. I've lost what is really important to me." Neely listened carefully, then said simply, "You never know that Jesus is all you need until Jesus is all you have." Then Neely told Leslie she could pray. "Start with praise and confession," she said. "Then ask for help."

Leslie didn't have many options left, so she tried it. She prayed for forgiveness for what she had done, for the pain she felt she had caused us at home. Afterward, she didn't feel any different.

Another sitter came to watch from three until eleven—another black woman who kept saying, "Praise the Lord!" Then Leslie's Aunt Sarah called. They talked for two hours—something that had only happened long ago, if ever. Like the rest of Leslie's family, Aunt Sarah was concerned about Leslie's involvement in our church, suspicious of a religious tradition different from her own experience. "What kind of church is this Stanwich?" she bristled. "What are they telling you?"

When the next nurse was assigned to Leslie, she was disturbed about it—just sitting in the dark from eleven at night until seven the next morning. Leslie heard her talking about it out in the hall. But the woman didn't comment when she came into the room; she just turned the lights on. Leslie couldn't sleep with the lights on, so she ended up praying all night—hoping all this was a dream.

In the middle of the night, Lois came by to pray with Leslie again. The unhappy sitter was listening, and after a few moments she spoke to Leslie for the first time. "You just ask the Lord," she said, "and He will give you strength." Now visibly changed, the woman continued to give words of advice and comfort for the rest of her shift.

On Tuesday morning, Lois came by and brought Leslie a copy of Andrew Murray's book *Absolute Surrender*. As Lois was leaving, the phone rang, and Leslie heard her father's voice for the first time in eighteen months. That didn't go well. He hung up, and Leslie's mother called back with words of accusation: "You obviously don't care about anyone but yourself!" Somehow Leslie was able to ignore the cutting remark. Instead, she asked her parents not to come to see her; their presence would not be helpful now.

After her mother hung up, Leslie leaned back against the hard hospital pillow, amazed. For the first time since beginning her long, painful journey, Leslie felt a sense of peace about keeping distance from her parents. She felt she was finally setting some healthy boundaries for herself, finally beginning to do what she needed to do to heal and stay healthy.

The next person to sit with Leslie was Alice, the mother of a premature baby that Leslie had cared for a few years before in Soundview Hospital. But Alice had to leave for an appointment midway through her shift and was temporarily relieved by an orderly who just sat quietly, reading a book. Cousin Carol called, and they talked about their Aunt Sarah and the questions she kept raising about Stanwich Church. Leslie told Carol she felt she had to defend the church.

When they finished, the orderly was just quietly sitting in the chair. "You don't need to defend God or the church to anyone," he said. Leslie stared at him, speechless. Then he turned to the book he was reading and read something from it that said the same thing.

"What are you doing?" Leslie asked him.

"Reading my Bible," he said. "Whenever I get a break, I like to get into the Word." Then, softly, he began to sing some songs that were praises to God.

It was not until a half hour later that a light went on inside Leslie's head. She saw something—a pattern in all that had been going on, a message that had been acted out by a parade of people who had come into her room as though prompted by a stage director—some willing, some reluctant, some just doing their job, but all arriving as though on cue, delivering the same message.

These people were real. There had to be something real behind their actions. It was a realization that blinked on in Leslie's mind, like silent words just forming into a thought, a powerful recognition. *Look at everyone who's been with you, and listen to what they've been saying!*

Still it wasn't over. Leslie was just telling the black orderly about the light going on in her head when Alice returned. Alice heard what the orderly and Leslie were saying and told about her faith. And while Alice was talking, Alice's mother came in and heard them. She offered to lay hands on Leslie and to pray. She prayed a beautiful prayer in Spanish, which her daughter later translated. Alice's mother knew nothing about why Leslie was in the hospital, but she prayed specifically for peace, comfort, and hope for Leslie—the very things she needed most.

Suddenly Leslie was hearing a chorus of love where before there had only been cold, angry silence. Leslie realized she had been surrounded by the language of God and hadn't heard any of it until all these different people kept repeating it.

That was the day, right on schedule, that Leslie was transferred to Hillcrest, the place she had left a few months earlier.

Now Leslie was faced with the hard reality of going back to a place where she had experienced indescribable pain, loneliness, and loss of freedom. But now she had begun, however vaguely, to sense the necessity of learning how to go with God. Could she do it? Was the silent director working on this, too?

As the ambulance pulled up to the entrance of the acute care unit, Leslie's mind flooded with memories. The big door. The buzzing sound that unlocks it just before the door can be swung open. The big round glass enclosure for the nursing staff. Leslie felt the sickness again, felt the looks of the staff, felt what they likely were thinking. *Oh no! Not Leslie again.* And there was the same admitting nurse, looking like she recognized Leslie.

"Don't judge me on the past. I'm not in the same place I was before."

"We never judge from past experiences here."

The next day, Wednesday, the first meeting with the assigned psychiatrist took place. It was Dr. Davies, a man who expressed a commitment to the way of Christ. He looked at Leslie and observed, "There's a difference about you, Leslie."

The next morning, Leslie was dismayed to find her group therapy would be led by a woman named Cora, a social worker who had been involved in Leslie's program the last time Leslie was admitted. She and Leslie had strongly disagreed on a decision Leslie had made. Now she was assigned to Leslie's case. *More hurdles!* Leslie thought. But toward the end of the session, Cora said, "I see a big change, Leslie! There's real growth in you."

Then even Leslie could see the change in herself. She felt free to talk more.

That night Joan called Leslie, saying that Dr. Davies had phoned about plans for Leslie's discharge. It was the first time that the possibility of her not returning home to Pound Ridge sunk in. "There'll be no decision until Don comes home," Joan was saying, and Leslie realized more clearly the depth of what she had done by taking the sleeping pills. For the next three days she agonized over what would happen. She felt nothing else would matter if her new home life was in jeopardy.

Having just begun to pray about things, Leslie wondered how to pray about this. Finally she whispered, "God, I know that you brought Joan and Don into my life for a special reason . . . and you have made us into a family. I want to believe that you won't take that away now . . . but . . . God . . . I don't trust you!"

This kind of honest talking with God was a breakthrough for Leslie. So was the fact that there was no lightning, no thunder after her prayer, no angry punishment for daring to express an honest thought. Just the freedom to be heard, to be honest . . . and still to be accepted.

The next day was Friday, the day I had been convinced by my New Perspectives colleagues to reconsider my decision. Joan called Leslie on the phone. "Leslie . . . I've spoken with Don, and I have something important to say." Leslie prepared for the bad news. Then she heard Joan say, "You can come home. In thirty days we'll reevaluate what is best."

Leslie wept. Nothing else mattered. Later she wrote what she felt in that moment. "Nothing can ever be so painful or seem so hopeless or make me feel like I can't survive it . . . if I've made it through this!"

So Leslie actually began to tell everyone in the acute-care unit who had been supporting her of the good news she had just received. She started giving praise to God, as the people in Soundview hospital had done before she was admitted to Hillcrest. Leslie began to say, "There is a God!"

Dr. Davies said to Leslie, "Now we have to decide what program will be best for you." The question was whether Leslie was emotionally equipped to handle the difficult therapy of a special program for sexual abuse survivors. Should she try to work through those issues now in such a program, or should she just focus on a transition back to normal life? She had faced this question before. She knew the issues of her past abuse were affecting her ability to cope with life. Yet the anger and shame and guilt that went with those memories had always pushed her away from confronting them fully.

Leslie prayed all weekend. She knew the treatment team would be making their decision the following Monday. So she asked others to pray for her, too.

At ten-thirty the next morning, the head nurse called Leslie out of a group therapy session to say, "You're being transferred to a new program. You must be in the group in ten minutes."

This was Leslie's answer! It meant peace, reassurance that God really was with her in all this. It meant freedom, too! Leslie could go outside for the first time in nearly a week!

In her new program Leslie began not only to heal but to contribute. "I've learned that there is a God," she said, and she began to tell the others what had happened to her a few days before at Soundview Hospital.

She began to point upward as she spoke. Her finger had a little bend in it, admitting to the others the fragile belief in direction from above. Over the days that followed, the others began to respond, bending their fingers, too, but still pointing up, saying, "There is a God, Leslie!" The leader of the group even began to point her finger up, bending it a little as the others did. "Yes, there is a God," she said.

And that's what I saw when I came home from the Boar's Head Inn, when I went out to Hillcrest to visit Leslie. The door was the same. The buzzer was the same. The glass enclosure was the same. The rooms were the same. But Leslie was different. I saw in her face that she had managed to hear the silent whispering in her dark moment. That she really was beginning to see.

"Pops," she said radiantly, raising her finger and bending it slightly, "There is a God!"

On a Sunday morning four weeks after Leslie had returned home to Pound Ridge, she announced, "I'm bringing someone from Hillcrest to worship at Stanwich today."

"Good," I said, looking at her. "Who is it?"

"It's a guy from my recovery group."

That Sunday morning I looked down from the choir and saw a young man sitting beside Leslie. When Leslie introduced him to me at the end of the service she said, "I want you to meet Jeff."

"Jeff!" I said. "I have a son named Jeff. . . ." There was no mistaking his name.

The young man looked at me with a light in his eye. "I really heard the message here this morning. This was for me."

I was taken with this young man. He was about the same age as our Jeff was when he died. The fact that this Jeff was black was especially heartwarming to me. I don't know why, unless it was my memory of the black man at Sloan Kettering who had helped me so much.

On the road to healing we see the tracks of God in more and more things that occur—in the people around us who begin to see God in everything and who hear the silent language of God in the simple words that are spoken. We see God in the beginning sunrise on the face of a new Jeff. We see God in the things we once thought were commonplace. And in that attitude of life we know we are never alone.

But there are times when we want to be alone, in the quiet presence of the Lord of the Silence. When we go to the silent place, a place of deeper perspective, we find He is there. And we learn to communicate with Him, in the stillness of the night.

10

IN A SILENT PLACE

AN EASTER REFLECTION

"For everything there is a season. . . . a time to keep silence."

—The Book of Ecclesiastes

Everyone wants a silent place, a place to be alone, a special place, even if we go there only once a year.

It is up to us to find the silent places that set the stage for hearing God. Then life's most important events can happen. The things that cause epic history happen in the quiet places, the places that allow us to prepare for great battles, for receiving monumental ideas, or for receiving the peace that changes our lives.

The place I've found is historic Stanwich Congregational Church in Greenwich, Connecticut, where Joan serves as associate pastor with Neely Towe, the senior pastor. There is quiet power in this back-country Greenwich church, just twenty-five minutes from my home in Pound Ridge.

It is three minutes till one A.M. on Good Friday as I travel toward my destination, keeping my promise to spend one hour alone in silent vigil at the church. I slipped noiselessly out of my bed at 12:30, leaving my family sleeping. A twenty-five minute drive over a winding dirt road with a washboard surface forces me to slow down as I drive into back-country Connecticut. Even before I reach Stanwich I begin to feel the peaceful blessing on the land that is the unique heritage of the old Puritan way. It is like driving into yesterday.

Now arriving, I press the button that closes the car roof, opened on the way to enjoy the full moon lighting the road. Now I stand in voiceless moonlight in front of a floodlit church that stands out from the blackness of the sky. It was built in the days when people liked to let the white simplicity of their churches speak in a visual language. The silent old horse sheds have since been converted into gleaming white Sunday school rooms.

My steps will sound loud to the person already on vigil kneeling inside the sanctuary. He is keeping the vigil the hour before mine, so I enter slowly, consciously clothing myself with reverence as I enter the Presence.

In front of me, high above the platform, is a slender cross now draped in black. A light bathes the altar, and an outside light shines softly through clear windowpanes on the pure white wall inside. A crown of thorns and three cut nails lie on a bare table at the altar, and a cushioned kneeler invites me to approach the place of vigil.

The person I replace rises slowly, turns with a soft greeting, and is gone. His steps sound softly into the shadows of the sanctuary, then echo away prophetically on the walkway outside. There is no movement now except for a slight stirring of the black veil on the cross. The sounds recede to an occasional creaking of a floorboard contracting in the coolness of the night. I am the only one in the church, but I sense comfortably that I am not alone.

Time stops. Having no watch, I am not aware of the moving of the hour. This is my place, my moment, my rare privilege to let the rush of life leave me, simply reading Matthew's account of Christ's vigil, praying, or just waiting in silence. Now, looking at the carpeted floor, I wonder what someone would think if I stretched out, face down, spreading out my arms in the human image of the cross.

No, it would look odd, certainly a bit too dramatic, if someone should come. But no one will come at one-thirty in the morning, and slowly I find myself kneeling on the carpet, then leaning forward, testing my willingness to lie flat. After a long time I lie face down, and in the comfort of the still sanctuary I stretch out my arms, reflecting the cross above, and breathe a long, quiet prayer.

Now the silent language of the Lord comes to mind. I remember the isolated incidents of past years and realize now that they weren't isolated after all. They were part of a constant communication, unspoken but present.

I recall the countless times when I looked again before pulling out into an intersection and stopped short, protected, as a car whistled by that had not been in sight a split second before. The time in Amsterdam when the muggers were distracted by the literature in my pocket—religious pamphlets, but they thought it was money—long enough for a car to stop and help me. Or the time just a few days ago when I woke early in the morning, aware of a lingering message of comfort from a visitor in my sleep. These special times of recognizing a hovering protective Presence come back to me now as I rest flat on the carpeted floor.

But now without realizing it I have risen. I am standing up, looking at my surroundings with new eyes. The side wall has a huge pattern on it that I had not noticed before. The outside light in the yard has projected the panes of glass on the wall, showing the imperfection of the antique glass. These shadows make me realize that the light behind is clear, but the antique glass that looked unblemished in the daylight is full of bumps and waves.

I marvel at the message of light and human imperfection. We are like this glass, projecting ourselves instead of the light, letting only some of the light through. Still, the image created by light and glass together is unspeakably beautiful. And if not for the windows, who would see the light?

As my eyes search the wall I notice something way down in the corner of the reflection. There is the shadow of a head, looking up. Now, as I turn to look, the head moves. I am watching my own shadow on the wall. My thought suddenly becomes a new prayer of thanksgiving for being shown how I fit in, in my little corner of this huge glass tapestry. I am part of this history of light shining through human imperfection.

A car quietly pulls into the drive. In a moment the mystique of my vigil will be changed. Too soon, the next person walks quietly up to me as I look at the wall. My greeting softly punctuates the stillness.

"This is beautiful, isn't it?"

"What is beautiful?" he asks, looking at me, not yet tuned to the surroundings. There is silence as he looks.

"See there? The imperfection of the glass. The light behind it showing in from outside is clear. It's the glass that's imperfect."

"Oh yes. I see it now."

"And see down there in the lower left corner? That's me."

"Yes, I see you," he says, not yet understanding the message.

Knowing that my replacement has not spiritually arrived yet, I mention my experiment of lying on the floor, and the newcomer now seems to come alive with a new communion.

"Strange you should say that," he says. "I was thinking of that just now as you began to speak."

"That's good," I say, appreciating the new understanding between us, yet not wanting to say too much. I've been here an hour, and my friend has just come in from another world of roads and radios. Now he will have time, from two until three in the morning, to experience this silent power. But before I leave I look at the list of vigil people and note there is a vacancy from three to four in the morning. No one has signed up for that slot.

"My wife will worry if I'm not home when I said I would be," my friend says.

"Maybe it will be all right to have no one here when you leave," I conclude, tired now.

I leave, vaguely troubled, not resolving my dilemma of wanting sleep, but not wanting to break this special vigil. Will my friend stay anyway? Will the minister come back and fill the vacancy? Will someone else come who has been called?

But neither the sound of my muffled engine nor my tires on the narrow roadway drown the silent call within: "You are to return."

"You mean, turn around and go back now?"

144

"No, you will invade the time of your friend's vigil and rob him of his special moment."

"You mean, go home now and return at three o'clock?"

Silence.

"But I've done my part. I've kept my vigil."

Silence again.

The thought now of keeping someone else's vigil quietly anchors itself in my mind. I steal into my home, write a note in case Joan awakes, and leave it on the kitchen table. Excited now, aware of the rush of time, I scribble: "There is a vacancy in the vigil, so I've decided to return to take the 3:00 A.M. hour. I'll be back in about an hour and a half."

Racing back now through the moonlight, feeling the rough washboard road beneath, hoping to return before my friend leaves, I feel the urgency. Will he leave on time? Will no one be there with the silent Presence for a few moments? Will the light go out and the reflection be gone?

Slowing now to maintain a quiet spirit, I idle my car onto the grounds. My shoes tap along the walk in the stillness of the night. The sanctuary door latch clicks softly, allowing me to swing the heavy door, and there is my friend kneeling still, where I left him.

Sitting quietly now just inside the door, I wait until his time is up as I slowly shed the speed of time outside. My friend stirs, rises slowly, and turns to me as I move noiselessly to the place.

"It's you again," he says, wide-eyed.

"Yes."

"I tried out what we said. I stretched out on the floor."

"Good."

"I like this time of night. It's the time when no one would stay awake with Him."

"I know."

Then quietly he leaves. I settle down now, noting once more the imperfection on the wall and my reflection looking up. Now praying, "I don't want to see the imperfections on the wall, Lord. I want to see you."

The minister had told of once seeing a huge, silent angel towering over him late one night while on vigil, and now I look around at a creaking noise. But no one is here. Just me . . . alone.

Kneeling, I begin writing to capture this moment, writing all that comes to me. I do not notice the graying of the dark night or the slow dimming of the reflection on the church wall or the fact that my knees are becoming stiff as they hold my weight motionless in this attitude of prayer. How many times in my life have I written on my knees?

The three chiseled nails and the crown of real thorns are before me on the table. Touching the nails, then picking up the crown with an unspoken prayer, I place it lightly on my head. The thorns are too long and strong to press it down. Two thousand years ago a crown just like this was pushed down hard on another head, and now I feel the pricking on my skin. Time stands motionless.

Now, dimly, I hear the modern sound of tires just outside. I notice with surprise that only the faintest shadow remains on the wall. It has grown light outside, and I hurriedly collect the gift of many pages filled with words, not wanting anyone to see them. I am not sure what they say because they have been written in a unique Presence.

I turn and ask, "What time is it?"

"Five A.M.," she says.

"Then two people missed this opportunity."

"Two people?"

"Yes. I was here longer than I thought."

Leaving, I wonder whether I will return at noon for the Good Friday service. Not remembering the drive home, I return to see Joan waiting in the kitchen, an expression of relief on her face as I open the door.

"I was worried about you," she says, searching my eyes.

Now after a long sleep, I have awakened again, and I have made my way to the noontime gathering of the body of vigilants and others. I hear the words of the minister reminding me that

Christ was denied by His Father, betrayed by His friends, entrapped by His priest, ignored by His confidant, tortured by strangers, abandoned in death. A little note in the bulletin I now hold, way down in the same lower left corner, asks a simple question: "Were you there?"

Looking past the rows of people, I see the black veil on the cross, still moving slightly in the current from the air vents. The crown of thorns and the three nails rest there on the bare table. The projection of imperfect windowpanes is gone from the wall and the outside lamp is out. But now, even in the light of day, I can see the imperfection in the glass itself. There is the same small distortion in one pane, and there is another one, down low. In the middle of the night these little imperfections loomed large, as they do when projected on the walls of life itself. Looking through the glass quietly, I answer the question printed in the corner of the bulletin.

"Yes. I was there."

Another rest, and I have been drawn back again, ready to greet Easter morning in its brilliance. The sanctuary is packed with people. The black veil is gone from the cross, and the bare table has been piled high with flowers. There are so many that they spill across the tabletop, along the altar, and down around the floor in a tumbled profusion of white and yellow and purple and pink, crowding each other good-naturedly, just as the people are crowding, expectantly, to celebrate together.

Suddenly three trumpets send shivers of sound echoing through the room. Three glittering gold flares of light reflecting off the trumpets match the brilliance of high sound that rebounds off the glass panes above. A shower of eagerness fills the room as I look down at the silent prayer in the bulletin.

"I pray that this service may help me to comprehend the reality of what You did for me two thousand years ago"—or was it last night?—"and that as my eyes begin to open, my heart may be filled with joy."

Now, with eyes wide open, ears filled with a trumpeted triumph of sound, I "re-member" myself with Christ. I member my-

LISTENING FOR GOD'S SILENT LANGUAGE

self again with Him, recalling His instruction to consider the lilies. And there they are before me, all standing as quiet white trumpets, announcing something without words or music. Each white trumpet stands straight, bursting out six white petals, each flared back as though some explosion of sound had just rushed out, leaving six points of sunshine yellow standing there. A seventh point, solitary and white, projects quietly beyond the others with a still, small voice, declaring a silent message of simplicity, purity, and closeness, asking an unspoken question of me, as I draw nearer later to consider the lily closely. The people have left. Only the flowers and I remain. But I sense the well-known silent Presence and a compelling silent question.

"Are you here?"

"Yes. I am here, Lord."

I realize that we are all in solitary vigils in life, watching our beloved family and friends move on, listening to their fading footsteps, wondering what the next life is like, vaguely noticing our shadows fading, knowing that we too are being prepared for a new re-membering of ourselves.

And then a revelation breaks through—or a further unfolding of earlier revelation. Even as we stand vigil here, others are standing vigil over us in unseen communion above.

We who stand and wait are beginning to understand new truths, see new visions, hear new sounds, sense a new Presence beside us. We are beginning to understand the silent language that is being spoken to us always. And now we know:

In the ending there is beginning.

In the darkness there is light.

In His silent language, even the lilies speak.

Part Four

LISTENING TO YOUR OWN LIFE

A Further Word

A Voice in the Wind

"I am the way, and the truth, and the life."

—The Gospel of John

You, too, can find a place of silent power.

You can learn to see God in everything, to listen for His silent language in your life.

You can climb to a hilltop and catch a little more of the sun, a little more color. There you will catch the wind.

The wind grows more noticeable as you grow older. It picks up speed where it didn't exist a moment before and blows in such spontaneous ways—sometimes a gale, sometimes a gust, sometimes a caress, sometimes an almost silent breath.

Here on the wings of the wind God rides into your life, whispering His presence, catching your attention. He brings to mind other relationships that exist right now, because relationship on earth remains after the body is gone, even as the glow remains in the sky after the sun goes down.

This silent language of love, this voice in the wind, this undying presence is the unending gift of God that permeates earth and outlasts time.

This language of love never dies.

Summing Up

In addition to being a story about someone else's family relationships . . . this book provides prescriptions for renewal of your relationships and your life.

Life prescriptions

- Explore the lasting—and everlasting—nature of love.
- Get out of yesterday into a new way of life.
- Create a new relationship with your children.
- Get to know your parents all over again.
- Look through new windows when you lose your focus.
- Come home to love.
- See the meaning of life through someone else's eyes.
- Love by giving of yourself.
- Change your mind about what God is saying.
- Find freedom from loneliness in a silent place.
- See God in everything.
- Listen for God's silent language.

You can use the questions that follow to apply the prescriptions in this book to yourself, to help you write other prescriptions.

THINKING ABOUT THE STORY . . . AND YOUR STORY

The Beginning

1. What do you think the hospital maintenance man meant when he said, "See God in everything"?

2. Do you believe God speaks in the silent moments of life? If so, why do you believe this?

3. What are some times in your life where you've struggled to understand what God was trying to tell you or to see God at work around you? Why do you think these times were so difficult?

4. Do you believe that God is at work in every circumstance of a person's life? Why or why not?

5. Try to think of some practical ways that you can listen for God's silent language in your life. Make a list of at least three things you have done or would like to do to "hear" better or see God more clearly.

PART ONE: WHAT LOVE REALLY IS

Chapter 1 · Together on the Cliff's Edge: A Journey with Joan

1. What kind of hang-ups tend to spoil your plans and get in the way of special times with the people you care about? What would it take for you to leave those hang-ups behind?

2. How easy is it for you to break away for a "serendipity" when it doesn't seem practical or convenient? As a result of your attitude, what do you think you have lost or gained?

3. How would you answer these questions: "What is most important in your life?" and "Who is most important in your life?" List only three answers. How do your actions and decisions reflect these priorities.

4. Can you think of a "huge moment" in your life, a crossroads when your whole future hung on one decision. How did you decide? What has been the result?

5. If you are married, what is the particular mix of romance, growth, and companionship in your relationship at this point? What do you like about that mix? What do you wish were different?

6. Can marriage consist of romance, growth, and companionship at the same time? If so, how?

7. How do you remain close to people you love as they develop new interests? What is the key to finding a balance between intimacy and individual growth?

Chapter 2 · Only One Love: A Lost and Found Mystery

1. Where are you in your life? How many of your loved ones are still alive and close to you? How many have departed, either through death or some other separation? How have you handled the losses?

2. Think about the simple pleasures that make up your life, the pleasures that come from hearing, seeing, touching, breathing. Make a list of three you are especially grateful for. How can you best thank God specifically for these gifts?

3. What time in your life have you been most acutely aware of the power and presence of the Lord? What time in your life has God's presence seemed farthest away?

4. Do you believe that love never dies? If so, why do some relationships end?

5. What specific steps could you take to help your relationships grow rather than falter in times of stress and loss?

6. Do you think that issues in a relationship ever just "go away" without being hashed out and confronted? Why or why not?

7. What does the idea that there is only one love mean to you? Can you love God without giving something to Him?

Chapter 3 · Our Promised Land: What I Learned in the Jordan River

1. Reread Psalm 88. Think of a time in your life that the Psalm expresses most deeply. Now take a minute to get a mental image of Jesus down in that particular "pit" with you. What new perspective do you get on the love of Christ and the meaning of His life on earth?

2. What steps have you taken in your life to "get closer to God"? What has been the result?

3. What do you think about the idea that we can get closer to God, and to anyone, by giving up our own way, our demand to be right, our desire to be in charge? Can you think of an issue in your own life and relationships where you are keeping God at a distance by holding on to your own way?

4. Is it really possible for us to draw closer to God in our own strength? What is our part, and what is God's part?

5. Where, according to this chapter, is your Holy Land? What places remind you most of God's closeness? In what voices do you hear Him most clearly?

6. How do you feel about the statements on what love is and what love is not, as explained in Part One of this book?

PART TWO: A TURN TOWARD THE FUTURE

Chapter 4 · If We Are Patient, the Answer Comes:
A View From the Mountain

1. Make a list of the four or five most significant losses in your life in the past ten years. These can include the loss of a loved one, a move, a vocational change, a broken relationship, even a theft. Which of these losses do you still feel most keenly? Why do you think this is true?

2. Which of your relationships are more important than the others? If you consciously centered your life around the "absolute importance of relationships," what would change?

3. How do you tend to cope with loss? Which ways of coping are healthy, and which are destructive? Can some activities be either?

4. How can the act of writing be a way to understand God's silent language better? Can spoken prayer serve the same purpose? What about talking with a friend?

5. How can we get out of yesterday's hurts and difficulties? How im-

portant is this in improving your relationships?

6. Do you believe you can love someone after he or she dies? Do you feel the loved one is conscious of your love? How important are these issues to you?

7. Why is it sometimes easier to find a new outlook in a different place?

8. According to this chapter, how is it possible to let go of those we love?

Chapter 5 · Building Steps: A Father-Son Project

1. Can you think of a time when a shared project drew you closer to someone you cared about? Have you ever had the opposite experience, where a joint project seemed to push you further apart? What makes the difference?

2. Can you criticize someone's behavior without making a negative impact on the person? If so, how?

3. Can you judge a person without making a negative impact on him or her? Why are we told not to judge others?

4. Why is it so hard to keep from telling the people we love what to do?

5. How is God a good example of "hands off" parenting?

6. Who do you relate to more in this chapter, Don or Trevor? Why?

Chapter 6 · Right to the Water's Edge: Billie's Last Adventure

1. What is the impact on others when you serve them with an underlying motive to receive something in return? What is the impact on you?

2. Read Hebrews 11. What does it mean to you that your departed loved ones are part of a "cloud of witnesses"? How do you respond to the idea of maintaining a "present tense" relationship with those who have died?

3. This chapter says, "There is a great unwritten law. We understand *after* we obey." How have you experienced this truth in your life?

4. Can you think of instances in your life where the "issue of who is right gets in the way of what is right"? What happened? How was the situation resolved? How can we reach a point of perspective, in the midst of our pain, where we can focus on "what is right"?

5. Have you gone through an experience of having to make deci-

sions about a loved one who needs special care? What issues did this experience raise in your own life? What did you learn?

PART THREE: NEW WINDOWS, NEW VOICES

Chapter 7 · The View From the Train: A Cross-Country Pilgrimage

1. How comfortable are you with silence? Is there a "silent place" you go to find healing?
2. In what ways do you find yourself responding to life like your parents responded? In what ways have you made a conscious effort to be different? What has been the result?
3. This chapter says, "When we speak with commitment in our words yet without trying to change others, we make a spiritual connection. . . . This silent language lives within the language we speak and is the thing that really causes people to listen." How is this silent language related to God's silent language?
4. Describe a time when a friend or loved one spoke to you "with the wisdom or voice of God."
5. Practice "creative noticing" every day for a week. Get a notebook and a pen, find a quiet place, sit quietly for at least an hour, and then write down what you see and what comes to mind. Try doing this for thirty days.
6. A priest in this chapter says, "Relationship happens when we let God do God's work and we do people's work." What does that mean to you?
7. What can you do when you become stalled in life and don't know the reason why? What are some specific steps you can take to "see through a new window"?

Chapter 8 · Givers and Forgivers: Voices Among the Tombstones

1. Is all suffering a tragedy? If you answer no, when is suffering a tragedy and when is it not?
2. What do you think about these statements? Why?
   - loss of relationship is the prime cause of stress.
   - self-preoccupation is the prime cause of loss of relationship.
   - healing comes from renewing old relationships and establishing new relationships.
3. Why does the process of "sharing one another's wisdom" help us learn more about ourselves and about God?
4. Can you remember a time in your life when a "coincidence" re-

vealed God's message to you? How did you recognize the message?

5. How does giving thanks in the midst of painful events (not necessarily for the pain, but in the pain) affect our experience of suffering and loss? What does it have to do with seeing God in everything?

6. Why can achievement be a trap for people in our society? What is more important to God? How do you know?

Chapter 9 · One Crooked Finger: How Leslie Came Home

1. What are some of the emotional blocks that can keep us from hearing God's silent message?

2. Where does healing of our hurts come from? How can we help ourselves be healed?

3. How important is motivation in being healed?

4. Can you remember a time when God brought good out of your less-than-pure motives? A time when your mixed motives got in the way of a good thing?

5. What is the most honest prayer you can pray to God at this moment?

6. Whom do you relate to most in this chapter: Leslie, Don, or Joan? Why?

Chapter 10 · In a Silent Place: An Easter Reflection

1. Do you agree that "The things that cause our history happen in the quiet places"?

2. What is the difference between being alone and being lonely? Between being lonely and being a lonely person?

3. How do you break out of loneliness as a way of life?

4. As an experiment, try spending one of your quiet prayer times in the attitude described in this chapter, face down with arms outspread. Describe your experience.

5. In what ways do you think you are part of the "history of light shining through human imperfection"? Do you think that God has spoken to someone else through your life? Why or why not?

6. Have you ever felt you were "keeping someone else's vigil"? Did you do it voluntarily, or did you feel it was forced upon you?

7. After completing this book, what does it mean to you to see God in everything? To listen for God's silent language?